THE PATH TO REST

Seven Steps to Reverse Self-Reliance and Recover from Burnout

By Laura Mendenhall

"Rest isn't about doing less; it's about trusting God more."

Contents

CHAPTER 1: INTRODUCTION

This book isn't just a guide; it's a lifeline for those of us who have done life the wrong way—relying on our own strength, striving to keep up, and burning out in the process. If you've ever found yourself at the edge of exhaustion, wondering how to recover, or felt the creeping signs of burnout but aren't sure how to stop the spiral, this book is for you.

Behind the endless to-do lists, the packed calendars, and the pressure to keep everything afloat, there's often a quiet truth: we're running on fumes, doing too much, and doing it in our own strength. For years, I lived that way—pushing harder, thinking that if I just tried a little more, juggled a little faster, or worked a little longer, I'd finally achieve balance. Spoiler alert: it didn't work. It never does. Burnout isn't a sign of doing too much; it's a flashing neon warning that we've placed too much reliance on ourselves and not enough on God.

This book is for the moments when you hit that wall—physically, emotionally, or spiritually—and realize you can't keep living like this. It's for the mom who wakes up tired and goes to bed even more exhausted, the woman who's stretched thin by everyone else's needs, and the soul who craves rest but doesn't know how to find it. Burnout doesn't have to be your permanent address. Recovery and renewal are possible, but they require a new way of living, one that leans on God instead of our own over-functioning.

Life can feel like a symphony—sometimes the music flows with a gentle, restorative tempo, and other times it crescendos into a fast-paced flurry of action. The beauty is in the mixture. God is the conductor, weaving every note into a masterpiece. But when we try to control the tempo ourselves, it leads to chaos. The goal isn't to eliminate responsibilities or escape the fast-paced seasons altogether. It's about aligning our hearts with God's tempo and trusting Him to direct the music.

Let me say this clearly: this isn't a book about doing less for the sake of doing less. It's about doing the right things—the things God has called you to do—with His strength, His peace, and His guidance. Sometimes we're called to slow down, take stock, and rest. Other times, we're called to pick up speed and step into action. One pace isn't better or worse than the other; they're just different parts of the symphony. The challenge is learning to live in tune with God's rhythm, not the demands of the world or the pull of self-reliance.

If you've burned out—or feel dangerously close to it—this book will help you recover, rebuild, and move forward with intentionality and peace. We'll uncover the lies that fuel burnout, explore the warning signs, and learn how to live in alignment with God's calling. Through the stories of Elijah, Joshua, Paul, and others, you'll discover that God meets us in every season—in the rest and the work, in the quiet and the chaos.

Together, we'll sift through what God has asked of us and what we've picked up on our own. We'll lay down what isn't ours to carry and embrace the life God has designed for us. And as you step off the treadmill of striving, you'll find that His grace is enough to sustain you, no matter the season.

Rediscovering Rest

When I started our blog, *Love Fast Live Slow,* in 2013, it was with a heart full of purpose and a determination to help other moms (and myself) escape the endless hustle. The mantra was simple: love well and slow down. For years, it was like my steady compass, cutting through the storm of overcommitment. I learned to say no to unnecessary to-dos, set boundaries around my time, and focus on what truly mattered. It was life-changing—but as I leaned into living slow, I realized there was one critical piece I hadn't fully embraced: rest.

I don't mean the kind of rest that happens when you're so exhausted you crash on the couch for a Netflix binge. I mean the kind of rest God designed for us—a regular, intentional rest that prevents burnout and recharges us to do what He's called us to do. Slowing down was a good start, but without true rest, I was still carrying the weight of self-reliance, and it was only a matter of time before I hit a wall.

The truth is, my journey to living slow was messy, full of trial and error. I thought if I could manage my time better, I'd finally have the space to breathe. But what I missed was that living slow isn't just about saying no or simplifying your schedule; it's about making rest a priority—not only when you feel tired, but as an act of obedience. God commands us to rest not as a suggestion or a fallback plan for when we're overwhelmed, but as a preventative measure to keep us aligned with His purpose. Without rest, even the most organized, intentional life will crumble under the weight of self-reliance.

The Biblical Blueprint for Rest

In the Bible, God doesn't just recommend rest—He models it. After creating the universe in six days, He rested on the seventh, declaring it holy. This wasn't because God needed a break but because He was setting a pattern for us to follow. The Sabbath isn't just about catching up on sleep or taking a break from work; it's about recalibrating, recharging, and remembering who is truly in control.

When we ignore rest, we're stepping outside of God's design for our lives. We're saying, "I've got this," instead of trusting Him to sustain us. And when self-reliance takes over, burnout is inevitable. Whether it's work burnout, social media burnout, or the exhaustion of trying to juggle a million responsibilities, the root issue is often the same: we've forgotten that rest is a commandment, not a luxury.

For years, I thought I was doing it right. I slowed down. I said no. I focused on what mattered most. But it wasn't until I started digging deeper into God's Word that I realized living slow wasn't about pacing myself; it was about trusting God enough to rest. Rest isn't a break from the work; it's the foundation that sustains it. It's what allows us to steward our energy and fulfill the callings God has placed on our lives.

This book is the culmination of that journey—a roadmap to living slow and resting well. It's a 7-step guide to recover from burnout, reverse self-reliance, and embrace the rhythm of rest God has designed for us. These aren't quick fixes or empty platitudes; they're foolproof, biblical steps to rebuild a life that is sustainable, purposeful, and full of peace.

So, if you're feeling the weight of doing it all and wondering why slowing down doesn't feel like enough, you're in the right place. This is about rediscovering rest as a commandment and a gift. It's about learning to live in tempo with God, letting go of control, and trusting that His plan is better than anything we could ever accomplish on our own.

Rest isn't the finish line; it's the starting point. And when you build your life on that foundation, you'll find the strength, energy, and grace to do what God has called you to do—without burning out along the way.

A Personal Journey of Letting Go

I won't pretend that it's easy. For me, letting go of control felt like surrendering my identity. My "can-do" spirit, my ambition, my pride—it all screamed against the idea of slowing down.

In my mid-twenties, I carried an embarrassing mantra like a badge of honor: *"I'll sleep when I die."* It was a creed that fueled my overachieving tendencies. By then, I was already a veteran go-getter, determined to outwork, outrank, and outshine anyone in my way. Productivity was my love language, and achievement was my oxygen.

Looking back, it's no wonder I fell headfirst into the achievement addiction trap. My family is a lineup of high achievers. My dad, a West Point graduate, career Army officer, holds a PhD in Sports Science, has coached world champions in rifle and pistol shooting, and proudly displays not one but six collegiate national championship rings from his years coaching at the U.S. Coast Guard Academy. My mom, equally inspiring, earned her Specialist Degree in Special Education, won Teacher of the Year, and built a legacy of dedication and excellence in her career—even while stepping away for a year to care for my dad full-time during his battle with leukemia.

Naturally, their work ethic rubbed off on me, for better and worse. As a kid, I learned to equate approval with performance—good grades, good behavior, and a good attitude earned me the gold stars I craved. I still remember one pivotal moment in elementary school when my dad promised me a dollar if I could beat all the boys in the timed mile run. Up until then, I didn't think I had a "thing," something that made me stand out. My friends were more popular. My sister was skinnier. My brother was smarter. But I thought, *Why not try?*

To my surprise, I won. And not just once—I became the fastest runner in my class for four consecutive years. With each lap I finished ahead of the pack, my identity as *the mile girl* grew stronger. By fifth grade, the pressure to maintain that title was immense. I vividly remember the day a new girl joined our class and effortlessly caught up to me in the final lap. As I pushed my limits, she breezed past me and crossed the finish line first. I was devastated. I'd held that title for so long that losing felt like a personal failure. I replayed another classmate's casual remark—"You can't win at everything"—as if she held secret social rules I had somehow missed. And yet, my ten-year-old brain countered: *Why not?*

That mindset—that relentless striving to win, to achieve, to outdo—shaped much of my young adult life. It wasn't about mile times anymore; it was about grades, leadership roles, and accomplishments that could be measured, celebrated, and shared. My dad's encouragement to "level up" was good parenting—an act of love that inspired me to reach my fullest potential and see what I was capable of. But over time, I twisted that motivation into something else entirely. I began to place my worth in what I could do rather than who I was. Achievements became my identity, and falling short felt like a moral failing.

Worse still, this performance-driven mindset bled into my relationship with God. I began to see Him not as my loving Father but as a cosmic scorekeeper. If I read my Bible daily, shared the gospel with my classmates, and avoided obvious sins, surely He'd be proud of me. But if I skipped quiet time, cheated on a test, or let gossip slip through my lips, I imagined His disappointment weighing heavily against me. Subconsciously, I turned my faith into a works-based theology. My accomplishments became a way to "earn" God's love—a theological disaster of my own making.

The truth, of course, is that we can't earn God's love. It's a gift, freely given through grace. But in my striving, I'd accidentally removed Jesus from the equation and cast myself as the hero of my own story. I thought if I worked hard enough, I could earn the Creator of the Universe's approval, as if my meager gold stars could impress the One who hung the stars in the heavens.

This book is for those who, like me, have spent years striving, only to find themselves burnt out and empty. It's for the achievers who've been running so hard that they've forgotten why they started the race in the first place. Maybe your striving has been for survival—caring for a sick parent, raising children with extra needs, or juggling responsibilities you can't simply put down. Maybe it's been for approval, purpose, or sheer momentum. Wherever you are, this book isn't about eliminating responsibilities. It's about realigning with God and discerning what He's truly calling you to.

As we move forward together, know that there's grace for every step. God isn't in a hurry; He meets you exactly where you are, walking alongside you each day. Take a deep breath, unclench those tight shoulders, and let's begin the process of healing—one deliberate, faith-filled step at a time.

Welcome to a new way of living—one built on faith, anchored in peace, and liberated from the relentless grip of self-reliance. What lies ahead could truly transform your life.

CHAPTER 2: UNLEARNING EXHAUSTION

Do we have any perfectionists reading? If so, welcome—I see you. Many of us carry a deep desire to feel important, and that drive often shows up as a relentless need to make things just right. Maybe you've caught yourself thinking, *If something's going to be done right, I have to do it myself.* Sound familiar? That internal pressure to take everything on, to ensure it's perfect, isn't only about getting things done—it's the trademark of perfectionism working overtime.

At first glance, I wouldn't have called myself a perfectionist. I've always thought of myself as pretty laid-back—someone who can roll with the punches and keep things casual. But over time, I started to notice small patterns that hinted otherwise. For instance, there was the time I baked a loaf of sourdough bread for a friend, and while it smelled amazing and tasted fine, the crust didn't come out as golden or symmetrical as I'd hoped. Instead of gifting it, I left it on my counter and baked another loaf, determined to make one that *looked* perfect—even though my friend would never have noticed or cared.

Or the afternoons when I find myself obsessively vacuuming the floors—twice a day, if I'm honest—because even if the rest of the house looks like a tornado blew through, at least the dog hair and crumbs are under control. Somehow, I've convinced myself that maintaining spotless floors equates to maintaining my dignity. It's not about anyone else's expectations; it's about the invisible standards I've placed on myself.

I remember our first year of homeschooling—a mix of determination and sheer terror. With no teaching background, I was bent on proving—to myself, my family, and anyone who doubted us—that we could make it work. Our dining room became a Pinterest-worthy classroom, complete with whiteboards, songs, and colorful charts. I signed my kids up for every activity I could find, convinced we could finally "do it all." Adding to the pressure, my son's in-home therapist visited daily, and I felt desperate to impress her. I overcompensated with elaborate projects, fearing she'd see my inexperience. Beneath it all was the deeper fear: *What if I'm not enough?*

I worked harder, planned more, and overextended myself, trying to secure my worth through effort and perfection. Striving disguised itself as diligence, but it was driven by fear—fear of failure, judgment, and falling short. In the process, I lost sight of the heart of homeschooling: creating a space for connection, curiosity, and trust. Society applauds performance, and I'd bought into the lie that my value was tied to what I could do, not who I was.

It's not that I expect life to be flawless; it's that I have a hard time letting go of my own version of "just right." And don't even get me started on writing this book. How many times have I rewritten sections, tweaking every word like the fate of the world depended on it? My writing is supposed to be a source of joy, and yet sometimes I turn it into a battleground for perfectionism, agonizing over details no one else will likely notice. My easygoing personality? Turns out it hides an undercurrent of unnecessary pressure to get everything *exactly* right, even when no one's asking me to.

As if the internal voices weren't enough, the world around us does its fair share of adding fuel to the fire. Western culture, in particular, places a high value on productivity and success. If you're not juggling a high-powered job, a side hustle, and PTA responsibilities while simultaneously making dinner from scratch and planning perfect family vacations, are you even trying? The phrase "having it all" is often a smokescreen for doing it all, which can lead to stress and burnout.

For working moms, the pressure of excelling at your job while being present for your family can feel insurmountable. Whether it's an upcoming deadline or the subtle (or not-so-subtle) expectation to be available 24/7, work can push you to sacrifice your own needs for the sake of meeting professional expectations.

Sometimes the pressure comes from the people closest to us. Maybe it's a well-meaning family member who questions your parenting choices or the expectation to be the emotional anchor for everyone around you. Even if your family isn't directly saying, "We expect you to do it all," the subtle, unspoken cues can leave you feeling like that's exactly what they mean.

Elijah Under the Broom Tree

The story of Elijah is one of the most comforting and relatable examples of God's response to human exhaustion. In 1 Kings 19, we find Elijah at a crossroads—a prophet who had just experienced one of the most extraordinary victories of his ministry but was now utterly spent. This man had boldly confronted King Ahab, challenged 450 prophets of Baal to a spiritual duel, and called down fire from heaven in a dramatic display of God's power. In a single day, Elijah witnessed the undeniable presence of God as fire consumed the altar, the wood, and even the water surrounding it, leaving no doubt that Yahweh was the one true God (1 Kings 18:20-39).

You'd think that after such a monumental victory, Elijah would be riding high on faith and confidence. But life isn't linear, is it? Triumphs are often followed by unexpected valleys. No sooner had the crowd cried out, *"The Lord—He is God!"* than Elijah's world shifted. Queen Jezebel, enraged by the defeat of Baal's prophets, sent a chilling message: *"May the gods deal with me, be it ever so severely, if by this time tomorrow I do not make your life like that of one of them"* (1 Kings 19:2, NIV).

Fear gripped Elijah. The prophet who had just stood unshaken before an entire nation now fled for his life. He ran into the wilderness, not as a man of triumph but as one broken, frightened, and unsure of his place. Alone and overwhelmed, Elijah collapsed under a broom tree and uttered a prayer that revealed the depths of his despair: *"I have had enough, Lord. Take my life; I am no better than my ancestors"* (1 Kings 19:4, NIV). In that moment, Elijah's heart echoed the cries of so many of us who have reached the end of our rope, convinced we can't take another step.

What happens next is a beautiful testament to God's understanding of our humanity. God doesn't scold Elijah for his fear. He doesn't criticize his lack of faith or give him a motivational speech to snap out of it. Instead, God meets Elijah in his weakness with tenderness and provision.

As Elijah lay under the broom tree, an angel appeared. With gentle care, the angel touched him and said, *"Get up and eat."* Nearby, Elijah found freshly baked bread and a jar of water. He ate, drank, and lay down again. The angel returned a second time, urging him, *"Get up and eat, for the journey is too much for you"* (1 Kings 19:5-7, NIV).

God's response to Elijah's exhaustion was not a command to do more but an invitation to rest and be nourished. The provision was simple but exactly what Elijah needed: food, water, and space to recover. God acknowledged that the journey was too much for Elijah on his own and offered the sustenance required to continue.

This wasn't just physical restoration; it was spiritual and emotional as well. God was saying, in essence, *"I see you. I know you're tired. Let me carry you through this."*

Elijah's story is a vivid reminder that exhaustion isn't a sign of failure or weakness; it's a natural part of being human. Even the most faithful among us have limits. Elijah's journey teaches us that God doesn't expect us to push through on our own strength. Instead, He invites us to rest in His provision.

How often do we find ourselves in Elijah's shoes, running until we collapse under our version of the broom tree? We might not be fleeing from a queen, but we run from deadlines, expectations, and our own relentless standards. Like Elijah, we hit a wall and wonder if we can go on. And in those moments, God's response to us is the same as it was to Elijah: gentle, compassionate, and restorative.

Elijah's despair wasn't born out of a lack of effort; it came from striving without pausing to let God sustain him. It's a pattern we often fall into—believing that everything depends on us, that we can't afford to stop. But what we fail to see is that this self-reliance is a chain, one that binds us tightly and keeps us from experiencing the freedom of God's rest.

Isaiah 40:29-31 reminds us, *"He gives strength to the weary and increases the power of the weak. Even youths grow tired and weary, and young men stumble and fall; but those who hope in the Lord will renew their strength. They will soar on wings like eagles; they will run and not grow weary, they will walk and not be faint."*

God's provision isn't just for moments of triumph; it's for the valleys too. And like He cared for Elijah under the broom tree, He cares for us in our weariness, inviting us to trust Him enough to rest.

When Rest Feels Risky

Performance-based living is the idea that our worth is tied to what we achieve or how well we perform. It's the belief that you are only as good as what you do. For almost 20 years, I lived under this weight without even realizing it. I was running a race with no finish line, chasing validation from every corner—work, friends, even my own internal scoreboard. The stakes always felt impossibly high.

I'll never forget the day my body forced me to face the truth: I couldn't keep living like this. It started subtly—an odd, lingering fatigue that wouldn't shake. At first, I brushed it off. "Just a busy season," I told myself, ignoring the fact that I was so tired I had to start taking naps in the middle of the day. And not the indulgent kind of naps; these were the *I physically cannot keep my eyes open* naps. My arms often felt so heavy I could barely lift them, and not-so-uncommon ailments started piling up: headaches, dizziness, stomach issues, acne. One by one, I explained them away. Stress, hormones, dehydration—it all seemed manageable, so I soldiered on.

Until the day I couldn't. One second I was wide eyed and alert, and the next, the world had gone black. I passed out. That was my wake-up call—literally. I knew I couldn't ignore this any longer, so I made an appointment with my doctor.

Apparently, when you casually drop the phrase "I passed out" in a medical setting, it raises some red flags. They ran *all* the tests—heart scans, MRIs, endless bloodwork, you name it. The verdict? Likely anemia, but there was a curveball: my kidneys were functioning at just 55%. My doctor leaned in and gave her solution with the confidence of someone delivering a life-altering revelation: "Drink more water."

That's it? Just water? Surely, I thought, there had to be more to it. I felt like I'd been handed a Band-Aid for a bullet wound. So, naturally, I sought a second opinion.

Enter the functional medicine doctor, who took one look at my bloodwork, pieced together the symptoms, and introduced me to a term I'd never heard before: "severe adrenal fatigue." He explained that my body was completely out of balance. He didn't mince words—he said if I didn't start making changes now, I'd be looking at years of recovery. Years. He gave me a prescription that was equal parts daunting and baffling: a strict anti-inflammatory diet for six months, a laundry list of supplements, and—wait for it—*sleeping in.*

The first two parts of the prescription didn't bother me all that much. I can follow a checklist like a pro, so stocking up on supplements and adjusting my diet felt manageable—though let me be clear, gluten, dairy, soy, and sugar-free for six months was no small feat. Necessary? Yes. Easy? Absolutely not. But I had a plan, and I was ready to tackle it.

The sleeping in part, though? *Excuse me?* Sleep in? Who does that? Surely not me, a proud card-carrying member of the Overachievers Club. The very suggestion sounded ridiculous—like a cruel joke or a challenge to my entire identity. Productivity had always ruled my mornings. My worth was tied to how much I could accomplish before the rest of the world woke up. "Sleeping in" wasn't self-care to me; it was failure.

So, naturally, I resisted.

Instead of rejoicing at this seemingly divine decree to get more rest, I found myself… mad. Mad that someone had the audacity to tell me to skip my early mornings, the sacred time I thought was holding me together. I even called my best friend to rant about it. *"Can you believe this guy? He's basically telling me to give up the very thing that fuels me!"* Except it wasn't fueling me. My early mornings weren't the problem, but years—who am I kidding, *decades*—of over-functioning in the name of being a fully capable adult had taken their toll.

Here I was, physically falling apart, yet internally wrestling with the simple idea of slowing down. Somewhere deep down, I still believed I could outwork my exhaustion, fix my body with sheer willpower, and bounce back as if nothing had happened. But this time, my body wasn't just asking for rest—it was *demanding* it. And I knew I couldn't ignore it any longer. It was time to stop fighting and start listening.

Turns out, I wasn't the first to balk at the idea of rest. Remember Moses? After meeting with God on Mount Sinai, he came down to deliver the Ten Commandments, including one that must have sounded like a dream to a nation of former slaves: *"Remember the Sabbath day by keeping it holy"* (Exodus 20:8, NIV). Here were the Israelites, freshly freed from 400 years of relentless labor, and now God was commanding them to take a break. You'd think they'd throw a party, right? Wrong. Much like me, they bucked.

Let's set the scene. These people were survivors, conditioned to believe that survival depended on constant toil. Rest was a foreign concept, one that likely triggered more fear than relief. What if they fell behind? What if the food ran out? When Moses passed along God's instructions to rest, their first instinct wasn't gratitude—it was doubt.

In fact, in Exodus 16, before the Sabbath commandment was even etched in stone, God gave the Israelites a sort of "Sabbath preview." He provided manna each morning for six days, with a double portion on the sixth day so they wouldn't have to gather food on the seventh. It was a practical, tangible way to teach them to trust Him. But did they listen? Nope. Some of them went out on the Sabbath anyway, searching for manna, only to find… nothing. God's response was pointed: *"How long will you refuse to keep my commands and my instructions?"* (Exodus 16:28, NIV).

Can you imagine? After years of backbreaking labor in Egypt, here was a God who said, *"You don't have to work today. I'll provide."* Yet their fear of scarcity and their deeply ingrained habits led them to disobey. They were so used to striving that resting felt like a risk they couldn't afford to take. Sound familiar?

It hit me later how much I resonated with those Israelites. Like them, I had spent years in a relentless tempo, convinced that resting was dangerous, impractical, or even irresponsible. Here's the thing about the Israelites—they didn't stay stuck in that mindset forever. Throughout the remaining chapters of this book, we'll explore their journey and the lessons they learned about rest, both good and bad. They didn't get it right the first time, or even the second. But after 40 years of wandering in the wilderness, being refined and shaped by God, they finally understood the importance of resting in Him before stepping into their promised land.

And that's where the hope lies. If you feel like you're getting it wrong now—if rest feels unnatural or downright impossible—you're not doomed. Change is possible. You can get it right tomorrow, and the next day, and the day after that. It's a process, and while I pray it doesn't take 40 years, the beauty of God's grace is that there's always time to start fresh. Rest is a skill, a habit, and a commandment that refines us over time, and with every step forward, we get closer to the life God has designed for us.

When the doctor essentially told me to take a Sabbath for my body and soul—sleep more, eat better, stop striving—I didn't feel relief. I felt panic. Rest wasn't something I trusted; it felt like a trap, a setback, something that would leave me behind while the world moved forward. Just like the Israelites, I didn't want to stop gathering my metaphorical manna, even though the endless striving was costing me more than I cared to admit.

The Israelites had to learn—over and over again—that God's provision wasn't tied to their effort. It wasn't about how much they could gather, how hard they could work, or how perfectly they could plan. God wanted them to rest as an act of faith, a declaration that they trusted Him to meet their needs. And that's exactly what I needed to learn too.

So there I was, standing at the crossroads of surrender and self-reliance, facing my own version of the Sabbath commandment: slow down, rest, and trust that it's enough. And let me tell you, it's far harder than it sounds. Rest is about believing that God is in control even when you're not working, that the world won't fall apart if you take a step back, and that your worth has never been tied to how much you accomplish. True rest requires a leap of faith—a step into God's symphony that redefines not only how we rest but how we live.

As we move into the heart of this book, I want you to know I've written these next chapters with you in mind. My original manuscript included an additional 10,000 words, but I made the deliberate choice to strip it down for your sake. I didn't want this to be another book that feels like a project to finish. Instead, I crafted this as a resource you can take with you—a guide small enough to slip into your purse so it can move at your pace.

Whether you're at ball practice, in a waiting room, on your lunch break, or stuck in the car line, this book is meant to be your companion. Pull it out, read, re-read, take notes, and let the truths soak into your soul. I know you're busy; I know you're moving. But here's the thing: even in your hurried life, God is fully capable of piercing your heart and calming your spirit right where you are.

The next seven steps are tangible, transformative, and designed to help you reverse self-reliance and recover from burnout. These steps aren't quick fixes—they're truths to marinate on, apply, and revisit as you go. Together, we'll explore how to break free from stress, release toxic habits, and embrace God's sustaining peace.

"Burnout isn't just exhaustion—it's a symptom of misplaced reliance."

CHAPTER 2 ½: SETTING THE STAGE

I know a "half" chapter isn't a thing, but humor me. Before we dive into the seven steps, let's set the stage. If "steps" make you think, *Great, another checklist to fail,* don't worry. These aren't here to add to your burdens—they're here to help you hand over the overwhelm to Jesus, one piece at a time.

You won't need a degree in theology or a two-hour block of uninterrupted silence (because when does that ever happen?). What you will need is an open heart and a willingness to let God do what He does best: restore.

Here's what's included in each of the following seven chapters:

Step-by-Step Instructions: Each chapter will walk you through one step—why it matters and how to make it work in your everyday life. Think of it like a how-to guide, but with way more grace and no pressure to "nail it."

Real-Life Application: These steps are built for busy moms. You can start where you are, with what you've got. Whether it's sneaking in a moment of stillness between snack requests or saying "no" to that one thing you really don't have time for, you'll find practical ways to move toward peace.

Reflection Prompts: To help you process what you're learning, you'll have space to reflect and dig a little deeper. Don't worry—no essays required.

This isn't about turning your life upside down overnight. It's about taking small, intentional steps that lead to big, meaningful change. By the end, you'll have more than just a toolbox—you'll have a new mindset, one that makes space for God to take the lead.

A Sneak Peek at What's Ahead

If you're anything like me, your fast-moving mind is already trying to analyze what's ahead and subconsciously decide if this journey is worth your time. *After all, you've got to protect your margin, and does reading a book really count as a priority right now?* For my fellow overthinkers, let me put your mind at ease by giving you a glimpse of what's coming.

These next seven steps aren't random self-help hacks—they're deeply rooted in biblical examples of real people who faced the same struggles we do: weariness, burnout, and the overwhelming need for God's restoration. After studying rest and weariness in Scripture, I can confidently tell you this: these steps work. They worked for people in the Old and New Testaments, and they'll work for us too because God hasn't changed. He's the same rescuer, healer, and restorer, inviting us into His grace-filled rhythm of life.

As we move forward, here are the seven steps we'll explore together:

Step 1: Identify Your Gilgal
Step 2: Build Your Circle
Step 3: Stop Wasting Energy
Step 4: Be Willing to Give It All Up
Step 5: Live a 24-Hour Life
Step 6: Establish Better Habits
Step 7: Rewire Your Brain

If you're wondering what some of these mean (*Gilgal? 24-hour life?*), don't worry. Each chapter will break it down and show you how it applies to your real, everyday life. Some of these steps might stretch you; others might feel like coming home. All of them are here to help you move from striving to surrender, from burnout to breakthrough.

If there's a step that jumps out to you—one you're eager to dive into or one you're tempted to skip—feel free to jump around. Skipping ahead is fine if that's what you need right now. But skipping a step entirely because you think it's overdone or you've already perfected it? That's a red flag. Each step builds on the others, and skipping one could leave a critical gap. Think of it like assembling IKEA furniture: you might end up with something that looks fine at first glance, but it'll wobble under pressure—and you'll still have leftover pieces that make you wonder what you missed.

And if you think you've already mastered one of these steps, that's probably the exact one you need to focus on most. (I hate to break it to you, but that might be the enemy whispering, *You've got this all figured out,* as a way to keep you relying on your own strength.)

Lean in, take it step by step, and trust that God has something for you in each chapter. Whether you're beginning your journey out of burnout or you're ready to fine-tune your life to align with His calling, this journey is for you.

CHAPTER 3: STEP ONE IDENTIFY YOUR GILGAL

"Cool planes," a polite house guest commented, glancing around my living room as if trying to count them all. Fourteen. That's how many paper airplanes had taken up residence in my 10x10-foot living room during a recent football watch party. I knew because my friends counted them—like they were on some kind of scavenger hunt. At this point in motherhood, I clean enough to keep up appearances of sanity. Those airplanes? They were part of the beautiful chaos that is life with three active kids.

I need to get this confession out of the way (as if you couldn't already tell): I'm not *that* mom. You know, the one with color-coordinated bookshelves, magazine-worthy mantels, and a knack for turning empty mason jars into seasonal decor perfection. My decorating style leans more toward "lived-in" with a strong emphasis on "please don't trip on the Legos." If you see a throw pillow actually thrown, well, that's intentional design in my house. And here's the thing—I've made peace with it. My home may never grace the pages of Southern Living, but it's warm, welcoming, and unapologetically real. And that's the vibe I want people to feel when they walk through the door.

I've come to realize that everyone's version of a "home base" is different. For some, it's a perfectly curated space with flickering candles, stacked books, and the faint aroma of vanilla wafting through the air. For others, it's a bustling kitchen where kids are loud, life is messy, and love is palpable. Maybe your place of peace isn't even in your house—it could be a cozy corner of a coffee shop, a favorite park bench, or that quiet family beach spot you dream about returning to every summer. The point is, we all need a space where we can hit pause, breathe deeply, and feel recharged.

For Nick, my husband, recharging involves lively conversations, a heaping plate of spicy Asian food, and cheering on his favorite team with the intensity of someone who thinks the players can actually hear him. Me? My version of recharging is vastly different. Give me solitude, a journal, and raw cookie dough, and I'm golden. Bonus points if there's calm music playing in the background. The beauty of this is that there's no one-size-fits-all when it comes to rest. Your recharge recipe is as unique as you are.

As you read through this chapter, my goal is simple: to help you figure out what fills your tank and how to protect that space. It's not about comparing your sanctuary to someone else's or achieving some idealized version of rest. It's about finding what makes your soul exhale. Because without a place to recharge, whether physical or mental, we're all running on fumes. And let's be real, no one makes good decisions—or good memories—when they're on empty.

Carrying the Load When Everyone's Counting on You

We're not the first to feel stretched thin, and we won't be the last. Every generation faces stress, but how we handle it makes all the difference. Think about those nearing the end of their lives—they're not agonizing over messy houses or mismatched socks. They're cherishing relationships and the moments that truly mattered. Love, connection, and faith endure when everything else falls away.

God, in His infinite wisdom, made sure to model this for us. Even Jesus, carrying the weight of the world, stepped away to quiet places to pray and recharge. If He needed moments to reset, how much more do we? From the very beginning, God rested after creation, not because He needed it, but to show us that rest is holy. And yet, we resist. We charge ahead, convinced that slowing down means falling behind, ignoring the sacred invitation to pause, pray, and breathe.

One of the most powerful examples of a leader managing immense pressure comes from Joshua. Moses' trusted protégé, Joshua witnessed the miracles of Egypt, endured the wilderness, and eventually inherited the daunting responsibility of leading the Israelites into the Promised Land. The stakes were impossibly high: over 600,000 men, plus women and children, looked to him for guidance. It wasn't just logistics; it was a spiritual and emotional burden unlike anything most of us could imagine.

I can't claim to have faced Joshua's level of pressure, but I know what it feels like to have responsibility staring you down, daring you to falter. When I was 23, I went from secretary to Tradeshow Director of a publicly traded company with a million-dollar budget in one promotion. That's right—one million dollars. (To clarify, I didn't say a one-million-dollar salary. Wouldn't that be nice?) I walked into that role with big dreams and a bigger ego, ready to prove myself. But it didn't take long for the weight of the job to feel suffocating. Every decision, every detail felt like the difference between success and failure, and the responsibility rested squarely on my shoulders.

Like Joshua, I had learned from great mentors, but there comes a moment when no amount of preparation feels like enough. For me, it was a corporate event. For Joshua, it was leading an entire nation. The stakes may have been different, but the feeling—the pressure, the self-doubt, the overwhelming desire to get it right—was the same.

Joshua's Gilgal: A Sacred Pause

Imagine the scene: the Israelites have just crossed the Jordan River, hearts pounding, feet still wet from the miraculous crossing. Before them lies the Promised Land, full of enemies to conquer and battles to win. If this were a Hollywood blockbuster, this is the moment when the hero charges forward, sword raised, ready to take on the world. But Joshua? He pulls the brakes.

Joshua doesn't rush into battle or rally the troops for an immediate offense. Instead, he makes camp at Gilgal—a place that becomes a sacred pause for the entire nation. This wasn't about convenience or catching their breath after a long journey. It was about something deeper. Gilgal was where they stopped to remember who had brought them this far and renewed their commitment to the One who held the real power.

Instead of strategizing battle plans or running drills, the Israelites gathered to reflect on God's faithfulness. Maybe they swapped stories that their parents had passed down to them about the Red Sea, the manna, or that one time God provided water from a rock when they were parched in the desert. Joshua knew they needed to be spiritually grounded before stepping into their next challenge. He understood what we so often forget: true strength doesn't come from plowing ahead; it comes from pausing and plugging back into the ultimate Source.

Defining Your Own Gilgal

The city of Gilgal is mentioned 39 times throughout the Bible. If you're like me, biblical geography has never lifted you from your seat with raised hands. To be frank, I've never once said, "Did that Pastor just mention Gilgal, the city eight miles from Jericho? No way! I needed that reminder today." Gilgal may mean very little, if anything, to you right now. However, my prayer is that by the end of this chapter, you will become as giddy as I am about establishing your own Gilgal and it's recharging abilities.

Out of all the chapters in this book, this is the one I've been most eager to share. I am excited to share proven Biblical methods to refill your empty tank. Yet, I am equally intimidated to communicate the power behind this seemingly insignificant location in Canaan. Gilgal is more than a city. It represents a home base. It represents a place of rest and refuge. Yes, Gilgal has latitude and longitude coordinates but it's more than a literal piece of land on this planet.

As we read above, Gilgal is introduced in the story of Joshua. Moses mentions it by name as he gives his final address to the people. He tells them that they will cross over the Jordan River and pronounce blessings and curses in between mountains near a place called Gilgal (Deuteronomy 11:29-30, NIV). God directed Joshua to lead Israel in recommitment to Him before they entered their next life season. In Joshua 4:6-7, 20 (NLT), per Moses's instructions in his last address, Joshua directed a leader from each tribe to gather a stone from the dry ground of the Jordan River and build a memorial to God:

"In the future, our children will ask you, 'What do these stones mean?' Then you can tell them, 'They remind us that the Jordan River stopped flowing when the Ark of the Lord's covenant went across. It was there at Gilgal that Joshua piled up the twelve stones taken from the Jordan River.'"

Next, God told Joshua to reestablish the covenant of circumcision among the second generation of Israelite males. And *"they rested in the camp until they were healed"* (Joshua 5:8, NLT). Follow along, don't skip over this part. So far, we can see that Joshua set up camp at Gilgal, dedicated it to the Lord for future generations (12 stones), and took away the shame of bondage by physically reclaiming their identity as God's people (circumcision). Whoa. That's a lot in one day.

It gets better, if you can believe it. Up until this point, they had been celebrating Passover, the holiday of freedom, in the desert. Their promised freedom had not yet come to its completion, but they honored the holiday and the hope of the future. This first Passover at Gilgal, in the Promised Land, was sure to be a monumental celebration. The very next day, they "*began to eat unleavened bread and roasted grain harvested from the land,*" and no manna appeared from the ground ever again (Joshua 5:11, NLT). This was the last time they had manna – marking the end of a miraculous provision they had relied on for 40 years! God was now providing something new. They would get to live off the abundance of the land He had promised them.

If you can massage your brain and pivot with me as we begin the process of identifying your own Gilgal, you too can claim freedom and healing as you rest with God. It's important to note, first and foremost, that before Joshua took action to overthrow neighboring kings, he acknowledged what God had already done. He didn't rush into battle and charge forth with his own ambitions. He set the tone by giving thanks to God on how He had led them to this point. If we are truly looking to find rest and courage to conquer tomorrow, this must be the first step in our own lives. When is the last time you told God thank you for all the unpredictable plot twists? Those ups and downs are what have shaped you for this very season.

The second thing Joshua did at Gilgal that further strengthened its purpose was to make right what was wrong.

Joshua followed through with removing something that was separating them from fully identifying as God's people (in this case, circumcising all military-aged men to reestablish the covenant of Abraham). This covenant was established because God wanted His people to be set apart.

Take this example and evaluate if you have any secret sin that is separating you from identifying yourself as a follower of God. You can claim to be a Believer, but if you live no different than unbelievers, what evidence is there that God is worth your holy living? God is waiting to restore you once you unlock the doors and invite Him into all areas of your life.

And the third thing Joshua did at Gilgal that set the foundation of Israel's faith in God was to practice God's commanded rituals. The people joyfully celebrated Passover, as was established a generation earlier. We can model this discipline by committing to rituals that bring us back to a place of worship and reverence. This includes prayer, reading God's Word, and getting connected in a local church. These obedient behaviors will function as guardrails to lead us along God's best path for our lives.

Those three things re-established Israel's faith in God. Once we've duplicated the framework of Joshua's set up in Gilgal (giving thanks to God, pruning stubborn sinful habits, and adopting Godly behaviors that enable spiritual growth), then we're in a position to begin conquering our purpose in a sustainable way. After the Israelites did these things, God flicked the light to green and it was time for action. What happened next is a byproduct of how they were fully charged and ready because of their intentional time at Gilgal.

They conquered Jericho and returned to Gilgal. They defeated the Amorites and returned to Gilgal. They battled five southern armies, the sun stood still, and then they returned to Gilgal. They attacked and won against the Northern kings and they returned to Gilgal.

Do you see the theme? God had already assured Joshua of victory over all the land, but it still required a lot of effort, strength, and courage—and after every battle, they returned to Gilgal to reset, to refocus, and to prepare for what was next.

After each battle and victory, they returned to Gilgal. It was a place of safety, refuge, healing, and worship. It's as if every obstacle they overcame left their stamina depleted and their batteries emptied. They knew they had to come back to their charging station. Yet how often do we jump from task to task, week to week, trauma to trauma, without resting at our metaphorical Gilgal? Too often. This is what leads to burnout.

I'm guilty of this. Remember that big marketing event I mentioned earlier? It turned out that I put forth my best effort and never reached the peak of perfection. One time when I forgot to order hors d'oeuvres for the CEO's big client meeting, I was spinning my wheels trying to resolve the mistake, and to no avail—I couldn't fix it. My brain was frantic. My heart palpitations returned, and executives left and right were asking me what was next on the agenda, I could feel my lips moving but I was numb from internalizing months of stress with no outlet.

Unfortunately, this unhealthy pattern repeated itself for years. My work anxiety got so bad that I'd cry in the airport security lines knowing the next few days of travel would be paralyzingly uncomfortable and upsetting. My once anticipated quarterly reviews became suffocating as my boss threw out words like, "more travel," "more leads," and "more events." Years had gone by since that eager 23-year-old fireball convinced him that she was the girl for the job. Years of relying on my own strength, falling under the spell of secular "go big or go home" hype, and convinced that a paycheck and prestige would satisfy my longing for significance. I was coming undone.

Ralph Waldo Emerson once said, "The years teach much which the days never know." Now that's a smart guy. Since my corporate America days, I've put better self-care practices into place. I've simmered my workaholism and I've found what truly satisfies my tired soul.

Real-Life Application to Your Gilgal

Now that we've unpacked the significance of Gilgal in Joshua's story, let's talk about what it might look like for you. You probably don't need a literal pile of rocks or a ritualized Passover feast to establish your own Gilgal (though if that speaks to you, go for it!). Instead, think of Gilgal as a sacred space or practice in your life—a consistent, intentional way to refuel spiritually, emotionally, and even physically.

Here are some practical ideas to help you discover and define your own Gilgal:

1. **Start with Reflection**

Think about where you currently go or what you do when you feel drained. Do you have a space or routine that gives you life, or are you running on empty? Ask yourself:

- Where do I feel closest to God?
- What activities or places bring me a sense of peace and renewal?
- When was the last time I truly paused and recharged?

Your answers can help pinpoint what recharges you, even if it's not obvious.

2. **Find Your Physical Gilgal**

It doesn't have to be elaborate—just intentional. Maybe it's:

- A chair by the window where you spend five minutes praying and sipping coffee in the morning.
- A walking trail where you process your thoughts and invite God into your day.
- A quiet corner in your home where you journal or read scripture without distractions.

It's not about the size or aesthetics of the space; it's about the purpose it serves in helping you connect with God and reset.

3. **Build Rhythms That Restore You**

Your Gilgal isn't just a place; it's also a practice. Think about habits that can become anchors for your soul:

- Setting aside a non-negotiable Sabbath day or half-day to rest and focus on God.
- Pausing midday to take a breath, reflect on scripture, or simply be still.

4. **Evaluate What's Draining You**

Like Joshua removing what separated the Israelites from God, take inventory of what's separating you from rest and renewal. Maybe it's an overpacked schedule, an addiction to productivity, or even a need to say "yes" to everyone. Make room for meaningful rest.

5. **Commit to Return Often**

Just as the Israelites returned to Gilgal after every victory, make a habit of coming back to your Gilgal regularly. Whether it's after a challenging week, a personal victory, or simply because you need it, don't let the busyness of life pull you away from your sacred space.

Your Gilgal doesn't need to look like anyone else's, but it does need to exist. Life will always bring battles—whether they're in your home, your heart, or your workplace. But like the Israelites, you don't have to face them without first pausing to refuel. Your Gilgal is your opportunity to stop, reflect, and let God renew your strength for what's ahead.

Take some time this week to identify your Gilgal. It doesn't have to be perfect or fully realized—but it needs to be yours. Peace is waiting for you there. Will you make the time to receive it?

The Gilgal Legacy

Gilgal was a sanctuary for the Israelites where battles paused, hearts were renewed, and faith was strengthened. This habit of returning, recharging, and recommitting to God was essential. Long after Joshua's generation, Gilgal remained a symbol of renewal and divine strength throughout the Old Testament.

Approximately 200 years after Joshua first set up camp at Gilgal, the prophet Samuel gathered Israel at Gilgal to crown King Saul, saying, "Come, let us all go to Gilgal to renew the kingdom" (1 Samuel 11:14-15 NLT). This wasn't only political; it was deeply spiritual, a moment of unity and recommitment to God before stepping into a new season.

Approximately 200 years after that, Gilgal marked more pivotal transitions, like in 2 Kings 2:2 (NIV) when Elijah and Elisha departed from Gilgal before Elijah was taken to heaven. It became a place of preparation for Elisha's next chapter, showing us the importance of being spiritually fortified for what's ahead.

Even in Nehemiah's time, Gilgal was tied to restoration. Three hundred years after Elijah was taken to heaven, Nehemiah 12:29 (NIV) mentions those "from Beth Gilgal" helping rebuild Jerusalem's walls, demonstrating Gilgal's legacy as a place of renewal and purpose across generations.

What does this mean for us? In Scripture, the Israelites returned to Gilgal repeatedly after emptying themselves for God's cause, not only to rest but to realign their hearts with God's promises. It became a practice they carried forward, a legacy of faithfulness that impacted future generations. Your "Gilgal" is whatever helps you stay rooted in God's presence. Returning to this place regularly allows you to walk in step with Him and leaves a lasting example of faith for those who come after you.

Joshua's victories always led him back to Gilgal, his spiritual home base. Without this practice, we risk burnout and disconnection.

Reflection

Take a moment to reflect on what fuels you, what brings you true rest, and where you feel closest to God. Identifying your personal Gilgal isn't about adding another task to your to-do list; it's about making things right with God. It's not a "feel good" place where God gives you a pep talk and tells you how awesome you are. In fact, nowhere in the Bible does God tell us that we're the main character or that we should simply believe in ourselves. He's the main character. He's the hero.

Gilgal isn't about centering ourselves; it's about centering Him. It's a charging station, a place to refill—not with our own strength, but with His power. The world tells us to rest so we can feel self-empowered, but the truth is, real stamina and power come straight from God. Your Gilgal equips you to accomplish the next task or face the next battle, knowing you're not doing it in your own strength but through His.

Ask yourself:

1. **What is my current rhythm of rest?** Do I have intentional spaces in my day, week, or month to pause, reflect, and reconnect with God? If not, what's stopping me?

2. **Where do I feel most restored?** Is it a quiet morning on the porch, a walk in nature, or a cozy spot in your home? Where do I feel God's presence most deeply?

3. **What do I need to let go of to create space for rest?** Are there commitments or expectations that drain me rather than refuel me? Where can I say "no" to make room for what truly matters?

4. **What would my own Gilgal look like?** Think about what it would take to build a place or practice of spiritual renewal in your life.

When you create space for intentional rest, you align your heart with His purpose, and that alignment equips you to face the battles ahead with courage and peace. Take the time to find your place of restoration, where God's love and provision sustain you.

CHAPTER 4: STEP TWO BUILD YOUR CIRCLE

There comes a time when the "I can do it all" mentality comes crashing down, and for most of us, it's not a graceful fall. It's a full-blown, face-first, out-of-breath collapse. We think, "I can handle this. I've handled worse." Until we can't. Step two on this journey to prevent and recover from burnout is admitting a hard truth: you can't do this alone. And that's not just okay—it's essential.

I learned this lesson the hard way when my husband and I moved to Florida in 2011. At the time, the thought of building new friendships felt daunting. I remember thinking, *Why put in the effort to make new friends? It's scary and hard.* After all, I already had close friends in Georgia—friends who I'd known since college, who I adored and missed dearly. Why would I try to recreate that? Besides, my job kept me traveling 75% of the time, living out of a suitcase and bouncing between corporate events and meetings at my company's headquarters back in Georgia. The idea of putting down roots in Florida seemed not only unnecessary but exhausting.

Sure, I was open to making acquaintances. I'd smile at new people I met at church, invite them over for some girl time, or chat during social gatherings. But that's surface-level stuff. Inviting someone into my *inner circle*? That's a whole different ball game. It's vulnerable, it takes time, and it's reserved for the special few who already knew me deeply. Most of the other young women I met in Florida had flexible work schedules (or didn't have to work at all) and stayed close to home, which made my constant traveling especially isolating. Whenever they sent a group text to hang out, I was notoriously the one who couldn't make it.

I felt like a fish out of water, thinking, *Why put myself out there when I'm hardly here anyway?* Looking back, I see it for what it was: pride and self-reliance, plain and simple. I had convinced myself that I could handle life, work, and stress without leaning on anyone new. Vulnerability felt like a risk I wasn't willing to take. But, as often happens when we think we've got it all under control, God had different plans. And those walls I built so carefully? They weren't as impenetrable as I thought.

It didn't take long for reality to catch up with me. The constant travel, the stress of planning corporate events, and the relentless pace of life started to wear me down. Piece by piece, my self-reliance crumbled under the weight of exhaustion. I didn't realize how much I needed a support system until life threw challenges at me that I couldn't navigate on my own. It was in those moments—when I felt completely drained and vulnerable—that I finally started to hear God's quiet nudging: *Open your eyes. Open your heart.*

So, reluctantly at first, I began to reach out to the women I had once overlooked. Those surface-level acquaintances slowly turned into genuine friendships, and over time, they became what I can only describe as *framily*—friends who become family. These women were my lifeline during some of the hardest seasons of my life. They offered encouragement when I felt defeated, laughter when I needed a lift, and prayers that carried me through. Their love wasn't just nice—it was transformative.

Twelve years later, when my husband mentioned the possibility of moving back to Georgia for a new job opportunity, my initial reaction was to dig in my heels. I didn't want to leave Florida, not because of the weather or the proximity to the beach (which is reason enough to stay), but for the community I had found. These weren't just friends—they were God's way of teaching me a truth I had resisted for too long: connection isn't a convenience; it's a command.

Ecclesiastes 4:9-10 captures this beautifully: *"Two are better than one, because they have a good return for their labor: If either of them falls down, one can help the other up. But pity anyone who falls and has no one to help them up."* These relationships God's design for how we're meant to live—together, helping each other up when we fall.

Identify Your Support Circle

God's design for community isn't a suggestion. From the very beginning, we see it in His words: *"It is not good for man to be alone"* (Genesis 2:18). Yet in our modern world, we often convince ourselves that leaning on others is optional, maybe even a weakness. We hustle, isolate, and tell ourselves that if we work hard enough, we'll make it through on our own. But here's the hard truth: self-reliance might get you far, but it won't get you through. Life is too heavy to carry alone.

Maybe you're someone who moves frequently, someone with a demanding schedule, or someone who has been burned in relationships before. I get it—building a support circle can feel like one more thing on your never-ending to-do list. But the truth is, we're not meant to live in isolation. Even Jesus surrounded Himself with disciples, friends who walked with Him, prayed with Him, and shared in His victories and struggles. If the Son of God sought community, why do we think we can do without it?

Think about the people in your life. Who shows up when you're struggling? Who encourages you to keep going when you feel like giving up? And, here's the challenging part, who *could* be that person if you allowed them to? It's not always the people you expect. Sometimes, it's the acquaintance who becomes a confidant or the neighbor you've only waved to in passing. Often, it's someone God places in your path for this exact season, someone ready to walk alongside you.

But connection doesn't happen by accident. It means being vulnerable enough to let someone into the messy parts of your life—the parts where you don't have it all together. It means putting down the pride that says, "I've got this," and replacing it with humility that whispers, "I need help."

Building community might look like joining a small group at church, inviting someone over for coffee, or texting a friend, and saying, "I've been thinking about you—how are you?" The payoff? Those relationships will become the hands that steady you when life feels unsteady. They'll be the voices that remind you of God's promises when your own feels too shaky to pray.

And here's the beauty of a God-designed support circle: it's not about what you *get*. It's about what you give. When you open yourself to community, you're also creating space for others to lean on you, to share their burdens, and to feel the love of Christ through your presence. That kind of mutual support is what turns friendships into something sacred—a glimpse of God's love in action.

If you're hesitant, I encourage you to take one step today. Start small. Look around at the people already in your life, or pray for God to bring new connections. Let go of the excuses that keep you isolated and lean into the relationships God has prepared for you.

Moses: Strength in Numbers

If anyone knows what it feels like to carry the weight of the world—or an entire nation—it's Moses. Leading the Israelites out of Egypt, navigating decades of complaints in the wilderness, and handling constant disputes would wear down even the strongest among us. Imagine dealing with millions of people grumbling about food, water, and wishing they were back in Egypt. It's enough to make anyone want to give up—or throw the stone tablets.

Moses' humanity is on full display in one of the most compelling moments of his leadership: the battle against the Amalekites in Exodus 17. The Israelites were under attack, and Moses sent Joshua to lead the army while he climbed a hill overlooking the battlefield. Armed with the staff of

God—a physical symbol of God's power—Moses raised it high as the battle raged below. As long as his arms stayed up, the Israelites gained ground. But as anyone who's ever tried to hold something over their head for more than a minute knows, his arms eventually grew tired. The staff began to droop, and the Amalekites started gaining the upper hand.

The weight Moses carried wasn't just physical; it symbolized the emotional and spiritual pressure of leading God's people. Moses wasn't a superhero; he was human, and his strength had limits. Enter Aaron and Hur, two companions who saw his struggle and stepped in to help. They found a stone for Moses to sit on and stood on either side of him, holding his arms steady until sunset. Because of their support, the Israelites won the battle.

This moment wasn't about a victory on the battlefield; it was a victory of community. Moses didn't need to do it all himself. God didn't expect him to. Aaron and Hur weren't there to lead the army or take over Moses' role—they were there to lift him up, literally and figuratively, when he couldn't do it on his own.

Moses' story offers a profound lesson for all of us. No matter how capable or strong we think we are, there comes a time when we can't hold everything together alone. The strongest among us need support, and that doesn't make us weak—it makes us human.

It's a reminder that help doesn't always look the way we expect. Aaron and Hur didn't fight the battle for Moses; they simply held his arms steady. Sometimes support comes in the form of a friend who listens without judgment, a neighbor who brings a meal when you're overwhelmed, or a coworker who offers to take something off your plate. These acts might seem small, but their impact can be monumental when you're worn out and weary.

Moses also shows us the beauty of shared victory. The victory belonged to everyone who played a part. Without Joshua leading the troops, Moses holding the staff, and Aaron and Hur offering support, the outcome might have been different. When we let others into our struggles, we share the joy of overcoming together.

How do we apply Moses' story to our own lives? Start by looking around at the people God has placed in your path. Who's there, ready to hold you up when you're tired? Who can you turn to when the weight of life feels too heavy? If you don't have an answer right now, don't lose heart. Pray for God to bring those people into your life and be willing to let them in when they come.

And here's the hard part for some of us: you might need to ask for help. Moses didn't push Aaron and Hur away, insisting he had everything under control. He let them step in. If you struggle with self-reliance, take a page from Moses' story and recognize that you're not meant to do this alone.

Who are the Aarons and Hurs in your life? And just as importantly, who might need you to step in and steady their arms? When we embrace the community God provides, we discover a strength far greater than anything we could muster on our own. That's where true victory begins.

Real-Life Applications for Building Your Support Circle

I could easily list twenty tips here, but let's be honest—you've heard most of them before. I don't want these real-life applications to feel like more noise or leave you rolling your eyes at yet another suggestion to "join a club."

Instead, I want to give you ideas that are practical, doable, and maybe even a little unexpected. If you notice a recurring pattern in these suggestions, take it as a gentle nudge that this could be your fresh call to action. Sometimes the most repeated advice is the exact thing we need to embrace first. Ready? Here are five ways to start building the kind of support circle that strengthens and sustains you.

1. **Create a "Battle Buddy" System**
Think of a battle buddy as your go-to person for life's ups and downs. Text them when you need prayer, support, or even a pep talk. This relationship isn't about one-sided help; it's mutual encouragement. Start small by sharing a specific challenge or prayer need, and build a rhythm of checking in with each other regularly.

2. **Host a Low-Key Gathering**
Invite someone over for coffee, lunch, or a walk in the park—no need for a spotless house or gourmet snacks. The goal isn't to impress but to connect. Real connection happens when we let people into our unpolished lives, sticky floors, mismatched socks, and all.

3. Let Someone Into Your Real Life

Instead of hiding behind "I'm fine," invite someone into the mess of your real life. Whether it's folding laundry while you chat or sharing your honest struggles, vulnerability fosters authentic connection. The friends who stick around after seeing the chaos are the ones you can count on.

4. Ask for Help with One Small Thing

If asking for help feels awkward, start with something simple: a favor like borrowing an egg, babysitting for an hour, or grabbing an extra item at the store. Small acts of reliance help you build trust and break the habit of carrying everything on your own.

5. Pray for Connection and Act on It

Ask God to lead you to the right people, and then take action. Reach out to someone at church, join a small group, or reconnect with a friend you've lost touch with. Often, the people you need are closer than you think, waiting for you to take that first step.

Reflection

It's tempting to believe that leaning on others is a sign of weakness or that asking for help makes you less capable. But the truth? It takes far more courage to admit when you need support than to struggle silently under the weight of doing it all. Let's pause and look inward. Are you shouldering burdens that were never meant to be carried alone? Are you overlooking the relationships God has placed in your life to strengthen and sustain you?

Take a moment to reflect on these questions and write down your thoughts:

1. Who in your life has consistently shown up for you, and how have you responded to their support?
2. Are there areas of your life where pride or fear has kept you from asking for help?
3. When was the last time you truly felt connected to someone who lifted your spirit? What made that moment meaningful?
4. What's one step you can take today to invest in building or deepening your support circle?
5. How might trusting others with your burdens be an act of trusting God with your life?

Building a strong support system isn't about achieving perfection or seeing instant results—it's about following Jesus' example. Reflecting on these questions is your first step toward embracing the community God has designed for you. In the next chapter, we'll explore the hidden ways you might be wasting energy and how to reclaim it for what truly matters.

CHAPTER 5: STEP THREE STOP WASTING ENERGY

Life is exhausting enough without us making it harder on ourselves. Yet, how often do we find ourselves fighting battles that aren't ours to fight, overextending ourselves on tasks that don't really matter, and spending every ounce of energy rowing against currents we were never meant to face alone? You only have so much energy, and if you're not careful, you'll pour it into all the wrong places, leaving nothing for what truly matters.

This chapter is about one powerful, life-changing truth: you don't have to fight every battle, fix every problem, or carry every burden. The secret to preventing burnout and recovering from it starts with learning to conserve your energy for the things God has actually called you to do—and letting go of everything else. When we waste our strength on worry, resentment, or overcommitment, we end up exhausted, running on empty, and disconnected from the peace God offers us.

This is more than a practical lesson. It's a spiritual one. Energy management goes beyond scheduling your time—it's about faith. It's about trusting God enough to release what's draining you and relying on His strength instead of your own. Whether you're a mom juggling countless responsibilities, a professional trying to meet every demand, or someone who feels stuck in the relentless pursuit of "doing it all," this chapter is your invitation to break free from the energy-wasters and step into a life of intentionality and peace.

Before we dive in, I want you to pause for a moment and ask yourself: *What is draining me right now?* Those energy-drainers are keeping you stuck. But you don't have to stay stuck. God didn't design you to live depleted. He's ready to help you redirect your energy toward what truly matters.

Letting Go to Move Forward

The call came sharp and sudden. "Pick me up at the causeway," Nick's voice crackled through the phone. His tone was serious, edged with exhaustion, and I didn't hesitate. "What's wrong?" I asked, but the connection wavered, leaving me with more questions than answers. Tossing the phone aside, I wrangled our kids into their car seats. Each one squirmed like they were auditioning for Cirque du Soleil. Buckling them in felt like a mini workout, but my mind was racing faster than my hands. What happened? Was he hurt? Did the boat flip?

The Florida sun was relentless as I sped to the causeway—a long, narrow strip of road that bridges the mainland to a barrier island, flanked by water on either side. The familiar roads blurred together in my rush, the shimmering heat rising off the pavement only adding to my anxiety. When we arrived, Nick stood on the shore near the base of the bridge, a picture of weariness and defeat. His shoulders sagged, his face glistened with sweat, and his oars hung limply in his hands. Relief washed over me—he was okay. But as he began to explain, I realized just how drained he was, not just physically but mentally too.

“The current,” he said, his voice heavy with frustration. “I couldn’t fight it anymore. No matter how hard I paddled, it just kept pulling me back. I gave it everything, but I wasn’t going anywhere.”

Nick, his dad, and his dad’s friend set out on the sailboat that afternoon for what was supposed to be a straightforward journey—moving our boat from Clearwater to a new dock in Tarpon Springs, about 20 miles away. With good company and a steady wind, the plan seemed foolproof. They towed our dinghy behind the sailboat, ready for any small errands or shore stops, but mostly expecting a smooth day on the water.

As time passed, it became clear that the tides and winds weren’t in their favor. The leisurely sailing trip was taking much longer than expected, and Nick and I had evening plans he didn’t want to miss. That’s when he came up with an idea: he’d unhook the dinghy from the sailboat, motor to the Dunedin Causeway, and I’d pick him up there. His dad and his dad’s friend could continue sailing to Tarpon Springs, and everyone’s plans would stay intact.

Nick packed the dinghy carefully, loading it with an extra cooler, oars, and a life jacket—everything he thought he might need for the short trip to shore. Confident in his plan, he hopped into the dinghy and motored away, waving to his dad and his dad’s friend as they continued their journey on the sailboat.

But what started as a clever solution quickly unraveled. Just a few hundred yards away from the sailboat, the dinghy's motor sputtered, coughed, and died completely. Nick found himself stranded in the middle of the water with no working motor, a set of oars, and the wind and tide working against him. What had seemed like a quick and simple detour turned into an exhausting battle to get to shore—and a sharp reminder that even the best-laid plans can go sideways when the unexpected strikes.

The waves, seemingly mild from a distance, were relentless up close. Every stroke of the oars seemed to push Nick forward only to have the current drag him back. The sun beat down mercilessly as he paddled for nearly two hours, his arms burning with the kind of exhaustion that only comes from a battle you know you're not winning.

"I had to stop a few times and lay back in the boat," he later admitted. "My arms couldn't take it anymore." Despite his best efforts, the dinghy seemed to be at the mercy of the waves. He had managed to cut the distance in half, but the shore was still a daunting half-mile away, and every moment spent resting allowed the waves to push him farther back. Frustrated but realistic, Nick finally recognized he needed help. "I had to stop paddling," he admitted, his voice a mix of exhaustion and resolve. For nearly 30 minutes, he waved and tried to catch the attention of other boaters, determined not to give up. At last, someone noticed his distress and stopped, steering over to throw him a towline. In minutes, he was being pulled back to shore, the fight over, and his exhaustion finally met with relief.

As he recounted the moment he gave up the fight and allowed another boater to tow him back to shore, I couldn't help but see the parallels to my own life—and maybe yours too. How often do we paddle against the currents of life, convinced that our sheer willpower will be enough to push us forward, only to find ourselves exhausted, frustrated, and no closer to our goals? How many times do we waste our energy fighting battles we weren't meant to fight, too proud or too stubborn to ask for help?

Nick's story brought to mind another leader who knew the weight of overwhelming responsibility: Moses (yep, again). Chosen by God to lead the Israelites out of Egypt, Moses carried the monumental task of guiding a nation of hundreds of thousands through the wilderness. His role wasn't limited to logistics like ensuring food, water, and shelter—though those alone would have been enough to overwhelm anyone. He was also the people's judge, mediator, and counselor. Day after day, from sunrise to sunset, Moses sat in the scorching desert heat, listening to every grievance, dispute, and question brought before him. Each decision he made was crucial, impacting not only individuals but the trajectory of the entire nation.

The demands were relentless, and the emotional and physical toll of trying to shoulder every burden alone began to wear him down. It was more than exhausting; it was unsustainable. In the last chapter, we reflected on Moses during the battle with the Amalekites, when he had to get strategic about dividing his energy. Instead of holding up his staff alone, he leaned on Aaron and Hur to help him keep his arms steady. Similarly, when his father-in-law Jethro observed Moses' overwhelming workload, he wisely advised him to delegate responsibilities. Moses learned that he couldn't lead effectively by doing everything himself—he had to lean on others and trust them to share the burden.

Moses, like Nick paddling against the current, was pouring his energy into an approach that would eventually leave him drained and unable to move forward. Both stories serve as a powerful reminder that when the demands of life weigh heavy, it's not weakness to recognize our limits. It's wisdom. Whether it's asking for help, trusting others to step in, or learning to let go of control, God often calls us to stop striving in our own strength and trust Him to provide the support we need.

Jethro, Moses' father-in-law, had the advantage of an outsider's perspective. He could see what Moses, buried under the weight of endless responsibilities, could not. This pace would break him. Visiting Moses at the camp, Jethro observed the daily grind—long lines of people waiting for Moses to settle disputes, offer guidance, and mediate their conflicts. From dawn until dusk, Moses sat at the center of it all, the sheer volume of work stretching him thin. Jethro, known for his wisdom and practical insight, didn't hold back. With a tone of firm concern, he said, *"What you are doing is not good. You and these people who come to you will only wear yourselves out. The work is too heavy for you; you cannot handle it alone"* (Exodus 18:17-18, NIV). Jethro's bluntness was a wake-up call to a leader on the brink of burnout. He could see the cracks forming and knew that if Moses didn't change his approach, both he and the people depending on him would suffer.

Imagine Moses in that moment. He had seen God part the Red Sea, rain manna from heaven, and perform miracle after miracle. And yet, here he was, drowning in his responsibilities. Jethro's words must have stung a little—no leader likes to be told they're doing it wrong—but they were exactly what Moses needed to hear.

Jethro's advice was clear and practical: "*Select capable men from all the people—men who fear God, trustworthy men who hate dishonest gain—and appoint them as officials over thousands, hundreds, fifties, and tens*" (Exodus 18:21, NIV). These leaders would handle the everyday disputes and minor issues, allowing Moses to focus on the bigger picture—guiding the nation spiritually and seeking God's direction for their journey.

This wasn't delegation for delegation's sake; it was an intentional restructuring of leadership. Jethro's plan ensured that Moses wasn't stretched to his breaking point while also empowering others to step into roles of responsibility. It gave the people access to justice and resolution without overburdening a single person. By sharing the load, Moses could reserve his energy for the most critical matters—decisions that required his unique calling as God's chosen leader.

As Nick stood by the water that day, his shoulders still heavy with the strain of the fight, the scene mirrored Moses' struggle under the weight of leading an entire nation. Both men, though separated by millennia and circumstances, had arrived at the same humbling realization: they couldn't do it alone. For Nick, it meant relinquishing the oars, leaning back into the dinghy, and waving for help, trusting a stranger to tow him to safety. For Moses, it meant acknowledging that he wasn't the sole solution to every problem, allowing capable leaders to shoulder the load alongside him.

Nick's muscles burned as the waves undid every stroke, and Moses' spirit frayed as the people's complaints piled higher with each passing day. Whether it's the physical drag of water pulling us back or the mental strain of feeling like it all depends on us, the result is the same—our strength runs out.

The solution isn't to paddle harder or work longer hours. It's to pause, reassess, and seek the help we need. Both stories remind us that the strongest leaders and the most determined fighters are those who know when to release control and invite others into the struggle.

Real-Life Application: Redirecting Your Energy

Managing your energy isn't about doing less—it's about doing the right things and asking for help when needed. Here are five practical steps to help you identify energy-drainers and refocus your efforts on what truly matters, inspired by both Nick's story and Moses' wisdom:

1. Audit Your Commitments

Take 15 minutes to list out everything you're responsible for—at work, at home, in your relationships, and in your spiritual life. Once it's all in front of you, ask yourself: *What's truly essential?* Cross off or delegate anything that doesn't align with your priorities or God's calling for this season. Use the framework Moses adopted: handle only the things that require your unique touch and entrust the rest to others.

2. **Practice "The Pause"**

Before jumping into a new task or agreeing to another commitment, pause. Ask yourself: *Does this align with what God is asking of me right now?* Taking a moment to reflect can save you from expending energy on something unnecessary.

3. **Delegate with Grace**

It's tempting to believe, "No one can do it like I can." But Moses had to trust the leaders Jethro suggested, you too need to identify trustworthy people in your life who can handle some of your responsibilities. Delegating isn't shirking responsibility—it's freeing up your energy to focus on what matters most. Whether it's handing off a household chore to a teenager or involving a coworker in a project, embrace the relief of shared effort.

4. **Create Boundaries That Protect Your Energy**

Block time in your schedule for rest—whether it's prayer, a quiet walk, or simply sitting in stillness. Nick needed to stop paddling and Moses needed to step back. Setting boundaries allows you to recharge. Start by identifying one area in your life where you've overextended yourself and commit to scaling back.

5. **Replace Your Energy Drainers**

Sometimes, what drains us isn't external—it's internal. Worry, resentment, or perfectionism can eat away at your energy just as much as a packed schedule. Identify one thought or habit that exhausts you and replace it with something life-giving. For example:

- Instead of replaying worst-case scenarios, meditate on Matthew 6:34, reminding yourself to focus on today.
- Replace resentment with forgiveness, praying Ephesians 4:31-32 over your relationships.
- Let go of perfectionism and embrace progress, reminding yourself that God values faithfulness over flawless execution.

By applying these steps, you'll begin to redirect your energy toward what truly matters—what God has called you to in this season. Like Moses, you'll find clarity and strength as you let go of unnecessary burdens.

Like Nick, you'll discover that surrender and asking for help can lead you safely to shore. It's not about doing everything; it's about doing what God has equipped and called you to do, trusting Him with the rest.

Reflection

Reflect on these questions to identify where you might be wasting effort and how you can redirect your focus to align with God's plan:

1. **What is draining your energy most right now?** Is it a particular task, relationship, or mindset? Write it down and consider whether it's something you need to release, delegate, or approach differently.

2. **Are you trying to handle everything on your own?** Be honest: are there responsibilities you're clinging to because you feel like no one else can do them? What might change if you invited others to help or simply let them go?

3. **When was the last time you paused to ask God for guidance?** Are you paddling against a current without stopping to see if you're even headed in the right direction? Reflect on whether you're taking the time to align your actions with God's purpose for you.

4. **How are you guarding your time?** Do you have boundaries in place to protect your energy, or are you constantly running on empty? Think about one way you can carve out space for God to restore your spirit.

5. **What small change can you make this week to better manage your energy?** It could be as simple as saying "no" to one thing, delegating a single task, or spending five minutes in stillness before diving into your day.

Write down your answers and consider one action step you'll take in the coming days. Remember, this isn't about fixing everything at once—it's about starting small, trusting God, and making intentional changes that allow His strength to sustain you.

Managing your energy is a powerful step toward living a life of balance and faith, but sometimes, even our best efforts at delegation and rest aren't enough. Why? Because the real transformation happens when we loosen our grip on the things we think we can't live without—you know, like control, our perfectly curated schedules, or that one couch cushion your kids keep wrestling with like it's a WWE contender.

Step Four invites us into a deeper level of trust—a trust that says, *"Even if I lose it all, God's plan is still good."* It's not always easy to let go (especially of that couch cushion), but in the next chapter, we'll dive into what it really means to release control, embrace surrender, and find the kind of peace that doesn't involve wrestling anything—or anyone—for it.

CHAPTER 6: STEP FOUR - BE WILLING TO GIVE IT ALL UP

The things we hold onto the tightest often reveal what we trust in the most. Maybe it's a career we've worked tirelessly to build, a perfectly planned future, or even the way we've always done life. Sometimes, it's our kids – their behavior, achievements, and choices. We can become trapped in the belief that their performance reflects directly on us, making us look either successful or like failure as parents. These things give us a sense of control, a safety net when the world feels uncertain. But what happens when we're asked to let them go? Not just loosen our grip a little but completely open our hands, trusting that what comes next is better than what we're clinging to.

For me, the things I clung to most tightly were security, stability, and predictability. Years earlier, God had already started the work of pruning my heart, asking me to surrender my career as an idol. Then slowly, I let go of placing my kids on a pedestal that only God deserved. But now, He was after something deeper—my curated peace. Not the true peace that comes from Him, but the counterfeit version I had built around the illusion that I could control and manage everything. Releasing that belief felt like losing a part of my identity. Yet, He was gently calling me to let go of that false sense of control and trust Him fully.

We all have something we cling to, something we believe holds us together. We rely on these things to steady us, to validate us, to define us. But what happens when we're asked to let them go? What if, like the rich young ruler, we're called to give up the very things that feel like our lifelines?

The young ruler's story feels ancient, but it's achingly familiar. His encounter with Jesus wasn't just about his wealth; it was about his heart—what he trusted, where he found his identity, and what he wasn't willing to release.

The Rich Young Ruler

Here comes the rich young ruler, strolling up to Jesus like he's got everything under control. You can almost see him—well-dressed, chin held high, the kind of guy who probably never ran out of camel parking. His wealth and status weren't accessories; they were the pillars of his entire identity, the things that made him feel important and, let's be honest, probably a little untouchable.

With all the confidence of someone who just aced life's checklist, he asks, *"What must I do to inherit eternal life?"* (Mark 10:17, NIV). To him, this was likely another box to tick, another achievement to hang on his perfectly polished wall of success. But Jesus, in His classic way, didn't give the answer the man was expecting. Instead, He aimed straight for the heart, bypassing the ruler's accomplishments and cutting through the illusion that he was in control. What happened next would shake this man to his core—and if we're honest, it might just shake us too.

Jesus didn't waste time with flattery or small talk. He acknowledged the ruler's outward obedience, giving him full credit for following the commandments since his youth. Imagine the ruler's chest puffing up a little, thinking, *I've got this in the bag.* But then Jesus dropped the bombshell that exposed the truth of his heart: *"Go, sell all you have and give to the poor, and you will have treasure in heaven. Then come, follow me"* (Mark 10:21, NIV).

This wasn't about Jesus hating money or wanting to clear out the man's bank account. It wasn't a blanket command for everyone to sell their stuff and move into a tent. This was personal. Jesus went straight for the ruler's weak spot—his attachment to wealth, his reliance on riches as his safety net, and his belief that what he owned defined his worth. Those possessions weren't just things; they were the pillars holding up his identity and the bubble wrap around his sense of control.

Mark captures the ruler's reaction perfectly: *"At this the man's face fell. He went away sad, because he had great wealth"* (Mark 10:22, NIV). You can almost hear the internal monologue: *Wait, sell everything? Like, all of it? Even the vacation house? The camel with the heated saddle?* His sorrow wasn't about losing material wealth; it was about losing the life he had so carefully built around it. He realized that the cost of following Jesus wasn't just steep—it was everything.

And before we dismiss this as ancient history, let's get real. While most of us aren't hoarding piles of gold bars, we all have our versions of the rich young ruler's struggle. We cling to these things like life rafts, convincing ourselves they'll keep us afloat.

The rich young ruler's story is a mirror, reflecting the tension between the life we grip tightly and the life God invites us into. His sorrow is our reality when we're faced with letting go of the things we trust more than God. But here's the kicker: Jesus wasn't out to strip the man of joy; He was inviting him into something better. The challenge wasn't about punishment or deprivation—it was about stepping out of self-reliance and into the freedom of faith.

What are you holding onto? What's your version of the ruler's wealth? If Jesus asked you to let it go, would your face fall too? These moments of surrender aren't easy, but they're the crossroads where we discover the life we're truly meant to live. Because only in letting go can we find the freedom, peace, and purpose that come from trusting Him completely.

The Road That Strengthened Our Trust

In 2022, life felt steady. We were two years into homeschooling, and for the first time, it felt like we'd found our stride. The kids had settled into their routines, and we were thriving in the predictable waves of home life. It wasn't perfect, but it was good. Comfortable. Safe. I was even feeling physically better than I had in years. After months of working with a functional medicine doctor to resolve nagging health issues that had plagued me for almost a year, I finally felt vibrant, energized, and whole again. Life, for once, seemed manageable and smooth.

But as the months passed, my husband and I both felt a quiet restlessness, like God was gently tapping on the door of our hearts, hinting at something new. At first, we ignored it. Why disrupt the comfort we'd worked so hard to build? After all, weren't we exactly where we were supposed to be—healthy, settled, and thriving?

Yet the stirrings didn't go away; they only grew louder. It was as if God was saying, *There's more. Will you trust Me enough to find it?* Adding to the unease, we began to feel like God was gently uprooting us from the church we had attended, served, and loved for nearly 12 years—a church where Nick worked and where we had poured so much of our hearts and lives. It wasn't something we'd ever imagined leaving. It wasn't part of our plan. Change is hard, and my stubborn heart wrestled with the idea of letting go.

The decision wasn't just about comfort or familiarity; it ran deeper. For years, I had wrestled with what a church should look like when it comes to serving, loving, and supporting special needs families (we have a son who is on the autism spectrum). I asked my mentors, sought answers in the Bible, cried, prayed, and compromised what my intuition was telling me. We had countless meetings with church leaders, trying to find a way forward that would align with what I believed Jesus would have wanted for my son. But heartbreakingly, the conclusion the church came to didn't include discipling my son as we had hoped. It was a devastating realization.

Leaving wasn't easy, but we knew it was necessary. I needed to heal. After years of feeling like my family was a problem, like we were a disruption or inconvenience because of our neurodiverse personalities, I wanted to run away. I wanted to hide. I cried out to God, desperate for reassurance that, at the very least, He accepted us. The wound was raw, and the thought of starting over anywhere else felt impossible. Yet, in my heartbreak, I clung to the faint hope that God had something better ahead, even if I couldn't see it yet.

In the wake of such a heavy season, I found myself yearning for something—anything—that didn't feel quite so overwhelming. I wasn't looking for answers or clarity but I wanted a breather. So, when Thanksgiving rolled around, we decided to do something a little out of the ordinary, something that felt more like an escape than a plan. A road trip from Florida to Texas—a bold move for two parents with three young kids, a car packed to the brim, and a hope that snacks and sheer determination could get us through the miles. "You're brave," our friends said with polite smiles, but their raised eyebrows told a different story.

For us, though, this trip wasn't just about getting from point A to point B. It wasn't even about the destination. It was about the journey—the miles stretched out before us, the shared experiences along the way, and the unexpected moments that can only happen when you're stuck together in a car for hours on end. We thought we were going on a road trip, something to shake up our routine and give us a break from the emotional weight of the past months.

What we didn't realize was that this trip would become a turning point, a divine breadcrumb trail leading us to a future we couldn't yet imagine. It wasn't only a getaway—it was the start of something bigger, something God was orchestrating in the background while we simply tried to keep the kids entertained and ourselves caffeinated. This trip, though unassuming at first, would plant seeds of change that would take root and redirect our future.

The drive itself was remarkably smooth—a rare win for a family of five on a long road trip. Each leg of the journey felt like its own little adventure, and our first major stop was New Orleans. The city greeted us with a cold drizzle and a curious blend of smells that our oldest son couldn't help but comment on as we walked past people smoking suspicious pipes. "What is that smell?" he asked with the wide-eyed innocence only a child can muster. My husband and I stifled laughter, quickly redirecting his curiosity with a "Look! A street performer!"

We braved the cold rain and stood in line at Café du Monde, where the warm, sugary scent of beignets made the wait more than worth it. Watching the kids' eyes widen as they bit into their first fluffy, powdered-sugar-coated treat was pure joy—pure, sticky, powdered-sugar-everywhere joy. We waddled our way back to the car, sticky fingers clutching the leftover bag, leaving a trail of white powder behind us through Jackson Square. A hot mess? Absolutely. Beautifully memorable? Without a doubt.

When we reached Houston, our next pit stop, the excitement shifted to awe. The Space Center was a highlight for everyone. We wandered through the exhibits, tracing the story of space exploration. But the true magic unfolded when we stepped into the historic Apollo Mission Control Center—the nerve center for all the Apollo missions, including Apollo 11, which guided humanity's first steps on the moon in 1969. It was like stepping back in time—the original consoles, the hushed reverence of the guide's voice, and the sheer magnitude of what had been accomplished there left us speechless. Even the kids, normally buzzing with energy, were quiet, soaking in the history of this iconic room.

After our stop in Houston, we continued our journey northward to Waco, Texas. There, we found ourselves tucked away in a cozy tiny house beside a sprawling farm, the perfect retreat after days of travel. Our visit to Magnolia Market was nothing short of delightful. We indulged in their famous cupcakes, the kind of sweet treat that makes you forget the rainy weather for a moment. The boutiques offered endless inspiration, and even the kids were enchanted—especially when they ended up playing an impromptu game of wiffle ball in the rain. (Yes, the rain—our constant companion on this trip!) The scene was sprinkled with pure laughter, muddy shoes, and the kind of memories you don't mind getting soaked for.

We spent the rest of the week in Temple, Texas, surrounded by the warmth of family and far too much Thanksgiving food. The highlight, of course, was our annual turkey hat tradition—a non-negotiable event where I lovingly insist my dad don his turkey hat alongside me. It's equal parts hilarious and heartwarming.

As the week came to an end, we packed up and began our journey back to Florida. Our next stop was Mobile, Alabama, where the rain—our faithful travel companion—greeted us once again with a steady, unrelenting drizzle. Undeterred, we grabbed our umbrellas and ventured to the USS Alabama and the USS Drum. The massive battleship and historic submarine were captivating, offering an incredible glimpse into history and providing a perfect balance of adventure and education for all of us.

To cap off the day, we found a small seafood joint tucked away by the water and settled onto the covered deck, where a live band strummed soft tunes in the background. The rain continued drumming on the tin roof as we dug into heaping plates of fried shrimp, crispy hush puppies, and coleslaw so good it earned an audible "mmm" from everyone at the table. The warm, buttery aroma of fresh seafood filled the air, mingling with the salty scent of the nearby bay. Time seemed to slow as we sat there, soaking in the music, the food, and the simple beauty of being together.

Each stop, each bite of food, each stretch of road seemed to breathe life into our family. The car rides were filled with music, laughter, and quiet moments of reflection. Worship songs played softly in the background as the kids napped. The hum of the tires on the road created a soothing beat that seemed to whisper, *There's more waiting for you.*

The idea of full-time travel came up almost casually as we drove through another stretch of highway. "What if we sold everything and did this all the time?" I asked Nick with a grin. I laughed at the absurdity, but the thought lingered. By the time we reached home, it was no longer just a passing notion. It was a seed, firmly planted in my heart, and it began to grow. That road trip was more than a family adventure—it was a gentle nudge, revealing the beauty and freedom that comes with stepping into the unknown. As we unpacked our bags and settled back into our familiar routines, the call lingered in our hearts, impossible to ignore.

Goodbyes, Faith, and New Beginnings

The question Jesus posed to the rich young ruler—*Are you willing to give it all up?*—is one that lingers in the hearts of anyone standing on the brink of life-altering change. For us, it wasn't just hypothetical; it became real. The fear of stepping into the unknown, of loosening our grip on everything that felt secure, was overwhelming. Yet, in a matter of weeks, that quiet stirring in our hearts grew into a full-fledged leap of faith.

We began shopping for a motorhome, cautiously entertaining the idea of taking a family "gap year" to reset and reconnect. It felt surreal, almost reckless, to consider walking away from the stability we had carefully built. But as we prayed and planned, we realized this wasn't about holding onto backup plans or safety nets. This was about trust—trusting God to provide, trusting Him to guide, and trusting that He was writing a story far greater than we could imagine.

So, we decided to truly lay it all down. We didn't rent a storage unit to keep our things "just in case." We sold nearly everything—the furniture that had made our house a home, the van that had carried us on countless family outings, even the kids' bunk beds where so many bedtime prayers had been whispered. The decision was practical, yes, but it was also deeply symbolic. It was an act of surrender, an intentional choice to live with open hands and let God take the lead.

The hardest part wasn't letting go of the stuff. It was saying goodbye to the people we loved so dearly. Friends who had become like family, the church community that had walked alongside us for years, and the daily comforts of familiarity. Change is hard. It demands courage and a willingness to walk through discomfort. But deep down, we knew this was our family's best next step. It was time to give it all up—not just the physical things, but the illusion of control we'd clung to for so long.

Real-Life Application: Letting Go to Gain More

Being willing to give it all up isn't a reserved concept for the pages of Scripture or a dramatic leap like selling everything and hitting the road. It's an everyday challenge, a call to release what you hold tightly so you can receive what God has in store. Here are five practical ways to apply the lessons from Chapter 7 to your own life:

1. **Conduct a "Heart Inventory"**

Take a quiet moment to reflect on what you're clinging to most tightly. Is it financial security, a career, a relationship, or your sense of control? Write down the areas where you feel resistance to letting go. Ask yourself: *If God asked me to release this, could I trust Him to provide something better?* This self-awareness is the first step to surrender.

2. **Release One Small "Safety Net" This Week**

Letting go doesn't always mean drastic action. Start small. Identify one thing you're using as a "safety net" and loosen your grip. For example, if you find security in over-planning, take one day this week to let go of the to-do list and trust God to guide your day.

3. **Practice Open-Handed Prayers**

When you pray, physically open your hands as a sign of surrender. Say, "Lord, I give this to You," and name the things you're holding tightly. This simple physical act reinforces the spiritual reality of releasing control and inviting God to lead.

4. **Declutter Your Life**

Sometimes, our physical possessions mirror our spiritual baggage. Take time to declutter a space in your home or your calendar. As you let go of what no longer serves you, reflect on how God might be asking you to create space for something new—peace, opportunities, or deeper relationships.

5. **Take a Leap of Faith in One Area**

What's one step you've felt God nudging you toward but have hesitated to take? Maybe it's reaching out to mend a relationship or saying yes to a new ministry opportunity. Take one tangible action this week to say "yes" to God's leading, even if it feels uncomfortable.

Letting go isn't about abandoning everything; it's about loosening your grip on what's holding you back so you can step into the life God has designed for you.

Reflection

Remember, it's not about loss—it's about gain. When you surrender, you open yourself to blessings and growth that only come when you trust God to lead.

1. **What are you holding onto most tightly in your life right now?** Is it your job, financial security, or toxic relationships? Why do you think it feels so hard to let go of these things?

2. **If God asked you to give up your version of "security," how would you respond?** How would you feel if He asked you to release the very thing you depend on for comfort or identity?

3. **Have you ever experienced a time when letting go led to something greater?** Reflect on moments when surrender brought unexpected blessings or growth. How can those experiences encourage you to trust God now?

4. What small steps can you take to practice surrender this week? Is there a specific area where you feel God nudging you to let go or trust Him more deeply?

5. How does fear hold you back from surrendering fully to God? What truths about God's character—His faithfulness, provision, or love—can help you move past that fear?

Take time to sit with these questions and let your answers guide you toward trusting God with open hands. True surrender isn't about losing control; it's about discovering the freedom and fullness that come from placing your trust in Him.

The Bible is full of stories of people who were called to take bold leaps of faith, to trade the comfortable for the uncertain. When Jesus invited the rich young ruler to sell his possessions, it wasn't about the money; it was about the heart. Jesus was asking him to trust in something greater than his wealth, to believe that what he would gain far outweighed what he would lose. Yet, the young man walked away, unable to let go.

Faith is often described as a leap, and for good reason. It requires stepping into the unknown, releasing the life you've built for the life God is calling you to. It's scary and exhilarating all at once. And yet, every story of faith—whether it's Abraham leaving his homeland, Moses confronting Pharaoh, or Peter stepping out of the boat—reminds us that when we trust God with our "all," He shows up in ways we never imagined.

Sooner than later, we said our goodbyes, packed what little we had left, and stepped into the unknown. It wasn't without tears or trepidation, but it was full of faith. We weren't just giving up a house or a routine; we were laying down the belief that our lives were better in our control. And as hard as it was, we knew deep down that this leap of faith wasn't the end of something—it was the beginning.

CHAPTER 7: STEP FIVE LIVE A 24-HOUR LIFE

As we packed up our lives and hit the road, we thought we were signing up for a year of family core memories—a chance to reset, reconnect, and show off our budding RV skills (which, spoiler alert, were less "budding" and more "bumbling"). But what we got was so much more than road trip playlists and scenic stops. The next 18 months turned out to be a wild blend of epic highs and "are-you-kidding-me" lows, full of plot twists that could either deepen our trust in God or send us into a tailspin of stress.

Each day became its own story—sometimes hilarious, sometimes humbling—forcing us to embrace a 24-hour life. Think about five years' worth of life lessons and sanctification pressure-cooked into an 18-month period. Like the Instapot of edification, it was fast, intense, and often left us reeling. Control? That flew out the window faster than a map in the wind. Instead, we were left with an unpredictable schedule where trusting God wasn't a choice; it was survival mode, His grace showing up just in time, over and over again.

In this chapter, I'll take you through the rollercoaster of few lessons we learned, the grace we found in the chaos, and how we discovered that faith isn't built in the easy moments—it's forged in the ones that make you laugh, cry, and sometimes wish you had a backup plan.

The Jeep That Wasn't in the Budget

One thing became abundantly clear: the road doesn't care about your budget, your plans, or your pride. We had barely hit "start" on this wild adventure when we realized a critical flaw in our setup—Nick's truck couldn't be towed behind the Mendenhauler (yes, we named her). The RV might've been our new home-on-wheels, but the truck was supposed to be our trusty sidekick. Instead, it was now just a very expensive paperweight.

Enter the Jeep.

Buying a new vehicle was nowhere in the budget. Let me repeat that: *nowhere.* But as anyone who's lived on the road will tell you, RV life is a masterclass in flexibility—and often, in spending money you didn't plan to spend. After a lot of deliberation and a bit of math-induced hyperventilating, we caved and bought a Jeep. It was the kind of purchase you make while silently telling yourself, *This will totally be worth it,* even as your bank account sobs softly in the background.

The Jeep was zippy, reliable, and—most importantly—it towed like a dream. But then came the inevitable domino effect: if we were upgrading the Jeep, shouldn't we spruce up the RV, too?

This was where my inner HGTV host came out to play.

I'm not a crafty mom—I don't renovate, I don't "upcycle," and the thought of decorating anything makes me break out in hives. But the Mendenhauler was in desperate need of a facelift. Out went the old beige trim and in came simple, crisp white accents. I painted, replaced the kids' awkwardly-sized bunks with fresh bedding, and created a minimalistic vibe that said, "We're trying, okay?"

By end of March, with the Jeep ready to roll and the RV feeling like something we could call home, we finally hit the road. Our grand plan was to head west. The Rockies were calling, and we had visions of sprawling national parks and epic hikes. But, as anyone who's done RV life will tell you, "plans" are just vague suggestions when you're living on wheels.

It would've been nice if the unexpected Jeep purchase was the only plot twist. But, oh no, life on the road had plenty more surprises in store for us. We were rookies, blissfully unaware of how unpredictable this adventure would be. The good, the bad, the ugly—we were locked in now. We'd signed the lease, sold nearly all our belongings, and, perhaps most binding of all, shared it on social media (because let's be real, once it's on Facebook, there's no turning back without a side of public humiliation).

But despite the hiccups, deep down, we knew God was up to something. He was setting us up for lessons far greater than we could imagine—about Himself, about our family, and about who we were when the comforts of predictability were stripped away. And let me tell you, He didn't disappoint. Through every bump in the road, He showed up, shaping us in ways only a journey of faith could.

Tornado Warnings and Humble Beginnings

The first few nights of our grand RV adventure was supposed to be magical—a moment to roast marshmallows, marvel at the stars, and congratulate ourselves on being brave enough to leave our comfortable life behind. Instead, it turned into a crash course in humility. Somewhere in the heart of Tennessee, at 2 a.m., our phones lit up with a tornado warning. I sprang out of bed in a panic, wildly googling "What to do in an RV during a tornado." Spoiler: the advice wasn't reassuring. My husband and I debated whether to hunker down in the RV or sprint to the campground bathroom, which didn't seem much sturdier. Meanwhile, the kids slept soundly, blissfully unaware that their parents were contemplating mortality.

By the grace of God, the tornado didn't come, but that night changed something in me. It was the moment I realized RV life wasn't going to be a perfect montage of sunsets and s'mores. It was unpredictable, humbling, and entirely out of my control. And I hated that. I'm a planner – think color-coded spreadsheets, meticulously written daily checklists, and that unbeatable dopamine rush from marking things off. The idea of not knowing what tomorrow held made my skin crawl.

That sleepless night reminded me of something deeper: the illusion of safety we all cling to so tightly. We think if we plan hard enough, prepare well enough, or worry long enough, we can bend life to our will. But life doesn't work that way, and God didn't design it that way.

It's not a new lesson, but it's one I keep needing to relearn. Living one day at a time isn't just a catchy phrase or a serenity prayer; it's an invitation to trust God in the small, messy moments when nothing is going as planned. It's a daily choice to stop clutching at our own plans and start resting in His. And for us, that journey began in an RV, where every day felt like an exciting mystery, tied up with a bow of God's unexpected provision.

Now, if living minute by minute and surrendering control sounds exhausting, I get it. I spent the first half of that tornado warning drafting our family's "how to survive a natural disaster" plan and the second half shredding it when I realized I wasn't in charge. But here's the thing: when we let go of the need to control tomorrow, we make space for God to show up today.

As I sat there in the eerie silence of the RV after the tornado sirens faded, clutching a blanket and trying to convince myself that everything was fine, I did what any good Christian would do: I prayed. Not the calm, composed kind of prayer you might imagine, but the slightly panicked, "Lord, please don't let this be the end of us!" variety. God was in the moment with me, no doubt. But let's be honest—I wasn't exactly pulling out all the biblical truths He's instilled in my heart over the years. I was more focused on making it through the night.

It wasn't until much later, when the storm had passed and my brain stopped resembling a scrambled egg, that I started to see it. Our RV journey, as messy as it was starting to feel, bore some striking similarities to Noah's humble beginnings and his remarkable faith. Here we were, asking our kids—

and our extended family—to "trust us" with these emotional and seemingly irrational decisions, choices that felt deeply right but looked undeniably wrong from the outside.

I can only imagine Noah explaining his own wild leap of faith: "So, I'm going to build this boat... in the middle of dry land... because God told me to." The side-eyes and whispered doubts he must've endured hit close to home. While I was nervous about towing a Jeep and avoiding tornadoes, Noah was out there building a colossal ark, trusting God with every nail and plank, every confused glance from his neighbors, and every moment of doubt his family might have had. Trusting God often feels exactly like that—a path that doesn't make sense until it does.

Noah's story wasn't only about the ark or the flood—it was about obedience in the unknown, taking one step at a time when the end result seemed impossible to grasp. And as much as I didn't want to admit it, that's exactly what our family had signed up for when we decided to hit the road. Like Noah, we were learning to trust God every single day, through every unexpected storm, breakdown, or plot twist that came our way.

Noah wasn't an experienced boat builder and did not have a team of skilled laborers at his disposal. He didn't live in a world that made following God easy. In fact, Genesis 6:9 tells us that Noah was *"a righteous man, blameless among the people of his time,"* but those people were deeply corrupt. Imagine the courage it took to stand out as a man of faith when everyone else had turned their backs on God.

When God commanded Noah to build the ark, it was a test of faith. Noah didn't have a shipbuilding background or a fleet of tools. He had no idea how long the project would take, what the outcome would be, or even if he would face ridicule for undertaking something so outlandish. All he had was his trust in God's instructions and the humility to start with the resources he had.

Noah's story is one of perseverance through the unknown. He didn't need all the answers before picking up the first piece of wood. He simply obeyed, day by day, plank by plank. And in doing so, he demonstrated that faith isn't about knowing the entire plan—it's about taking the next step, trusting that God will provide what you need along the way.

God's Faithfulness in Every Detour

The unpredictability of RV life felt like a modern-day nod to Noah's journey. Just as Noah couldn't have foreseen the exact twists and turns of a global flood, we quickly learned that living on the road is a full-time lesson in rolling with the punches.

There were moments that felt like pure gold. The kids usually played outside from sunup to sundown, inventing games, getting gloriously dirty, meeting new friends and rediscovering the kind of joy that only comes when screens are swapped for fresh air. We met other full-time RV families, and for the first time in a long time, we didn't feel like outliers. These people were quirky, adventurous, and beautifully unconventional—just like us. They became our tribe. We shared meals, stories, and even impromptu worship services.

One unforgettable evening, under a sky scattered with stars, we celebrated Nick's 40th birthday in true RV fashion. The kids had spent the entire day running around with the children of a few neighboring families. Inspired by their easy camaraderie, I decided to extend an invitation to the parents. "Come by tonight," I said, "We're throwing a party for Nick." Strangers though they were, they seemed nice enough, and hey, we were all parked together in this transient village of wheels—why not?

The RV was decked out with all the festivity I could muster. Streamers hung from the ceiling, fairy lights twinkled inside and out, and a humble but heartfelt spread was laid out on the picnic table outside our awning. Someone brought over an Oreo ice cream cake (bless their soul), and soon we were all gathered, stuffing ourselves and laughing like old friends.

Then came the music. Someone pulled out a guitar, another unpacked bongo drums, and before long, a spontaneous worship session broke out under the stars. The kids swayed in the background, the younger ones dozing off in laps, as we lifted our voices in unison. It was a moment of unplanned perfection—a reminder of how God creates community in the most unexpected places.

That night was more than a birthday party; it was a balm for weary souls. Strangers became friends, laughter became worship, and a simple gathering transformed into a sacred moment of connection. It was a snapshot of the beauty we'd been longing for: the reminder that even on the road, far from the familiar, God shows up in the details and stitches together lives in the most healing ways.

The Challenges That Made Us Question Everything

Like anything in life, with the highs came the lows. And, oh, the lows. Running low on money was a recurring theme. Living within a budget is one thing; living within a budget when your home doubles as a vehicle prone to breakdowns is another entirely.

Then there was the time our brakes caught on fire. Yes, you read that correctly.

If you've never driven a 40-foot motorhome through a crowded city, let me paint a picture: imagine piloting a whale on wheels through a parking lot designed for compact cars. That's the kind of day we were having when the Mendenhauler decided to up the ante with a side of flames.

We had recently picked up the RV from the shop after a three-month staycation with his parents in Atlanta. Among other fixes, they'd replaced the brake pads. So, when we hit the road and noticed the hot, acrid smell of burning brakes, Nick called the mechanics. "Totally normal for new pads," they reassured us. It made sense—until it didn't.

A few days later, the smell returned with a vengeance. Nick pulled over, and this time, there was smoke. Actual smoke. Note: This is not part of the 'new brake protocol.' Nick called the mechanic back. Their advice? Cool them down and head back their way. Easy, right? Not so much. The shop was in South Carolina and we were in Florida by this point, on our way to Disneyworld as a matter of fact.

As we carefully navigated through traffic, searching for a safe spot to pull over, the situation escalated. Smoke turned into billowing clouds, and Nick, ever the picture of calm under pressure, steered the Mendenhauler into the back corner of a shopping center parking lot where a cluster of open spaces awaited. He eased the RV to a stop, stepped out, and walked around to the right side and said "There are flames." FLAMES. While my brain screamed *Mayday! Mayday!* and envisioned the Mendenhauler exploding in cinematic fashion, Nick remained unnervingly calm. "Grab me some water," he said, like he was asking for a refill at dinner.

I sprang into action—or something resembling it—and grabbed the first liquid I could find: a cup of blue Gatorade. Yes, friends, I threw him a sports drink to extinguish the flames licking at our RV's tire. Meanwhile, the kids watched from their seats, completely unfazed, probably wondering if we were inventing some new road trip game.

Once the Gatorade made its dramatic debut, I sprinted to the fridge, yanked out every bottle of water I could find, and dashed outside. By the time I got to Nick, the flames were out, leaving behind a charred, smoldering mess and the distinct scent of my dignity burning alongside the brakes. I plopped down on the curb, head in hands, muttering, "Of course. Of course this would happen."

We sat there in silence for a moment, the enormity of yet another setback sinking in. The RV wasn't drivable, and we had to navigate our way back to the shop. But in typical road-life fashion, there wasn't much time to wallow. The kids were asking questions, the day was moving forward, and, somehow, so were we.

This was a reminder of what this journey was all about. Living on the road wasn't just about adventure; it was about faith. It was about taking each day, each plot twist, as it came and choosing to trust that God had a plan—even when our plans went up in smoke, quite literally.

And as frustrating as these setbacks were, they forced us to depend on Him more fully. With every repair, every obstacle, every curveball, we learned that surrender wasn't a one-time act. It was a daily decision, sometimes an hourly one.

RV life, much like life in general, was full of surprises—some wonderful, some fiery. But in those moments of chaos, God showed us that His provision doesn't falter, even when our brakes do.

Trusting God, One Day at a Time

Through all the unpredictability, one thing became abundantly clear: God doesn't waste a moment. Whether we were marveling at awe-inspiring sights – like majestic national parks or serene lake sunsets in Amish country– or lamenting yet another unexpected expense. He was present, teaching us to trust Him one day at a time. It reminded me of Noah swinging his hammer under the scorching sun, day after day, while everyone around him probably thought he was crazy.

Let's circle back to Noah. His story is a masterclass in living a 24-hour life. Imagine the scene: God tells Noah to build a giant boat because a flood is coming—a flood that would wipe out everything and everyone who didn't seek refuge on that very ark (Genesis 6:13-14). There was no rain in sight, no clouds gathering ominously, just an extraordinary command to prepare for something he couldn't yet see.

Noah didn't have the luxury of a project timeline or a detailed weather forecast. What he had was a monumental task, a few instructions, and a promise from God. And so, day by day, one hammer swing at a time, he obeyed. Each morning, he woke up, gathered his tools, and worked on the ark while enduring ridicule from his neighbors. "What flood, Noah? You've lost it!" I imagine the laughter echoing as he wiped sweat from his brow, quietly reminding himself of God's directions.

The work wasn't glamorous. Building a massive ark with primitive tools must have been backbreaking, soul-stretching labor. And let's not forget the logistics—gathering materials, ensuring the structure would hold, and eventually, herding pairs of animals onto the boat. All of this was done in faith, one nail and one plank at a time, with no tangible evidence that his effort would pay off.

Noah's faith wasn't passive; it was active, gritty, and relentless. Every day, he faced the same choice: to believe in God's promises or to give in to doubt and exhaustion. He chose faith, and his obedience became the bridge between

God's warning and God's deliverance. The rains did come, just as God said they would, and Noah's faith was validated as the ark became the lifeline for his family and creation.

Our own RV journey felt like a faint echo of that story. While we weren't building an ark, we were piecing together a life that required daily trust in God's provision and promises. Some days, it was the small things—finding an open campsite at the last minute or meeting kind strangers who felt like family. Other days, it was the big, scary moments, like smoke pouring from the brakes or mysterious water leaks behind the fridge.

Just like Noah, we didn't know what the next day would hold. We only knew that God had called us into this and promised to sustain us along the way. It was humbling and exhausting and awe-inspiring all at once. We prayed, we trusted, and we took one step—or one mile—at a time, learning that living a 24-hour life isn't about having all the answers; it's about trusting the One who does.

Noah's obedience reminds us that faith isn't built in one grand gesture. It's constructed in the daily choices to trust, obey, and believe that God's promises are reliable—even when they feel distant or impossiblets and in the small, steady steps along the way.

Real-Life Application: Embracing the 24-Hour Life

Living a 24-hour life means loosening our grip on tomorrow and trusting God with the details we can't see. It's not about abandoning responsibility but recognizing that we were never designed to shoulder the burden of the unknown. Jesus Himself offers this wisdom in *Matthew 6:34*: *"Therefore do not worry about tomorrow, for tomorrow will worry about itself. Each day has enough trouble of its own."*

When we lay down our need to know what tomorrow holds, we release the grip of self-reliance and embrace the freedom God intends for us. It's like letting go of the "calendar security blanket" that gives us the illusion of control. Instead, we live a life that boldly proclaims, *"If God gives me tomorrow, I'll tackle tomorrow's problems tomorrow."* This mindset not only deepens our trust in Him but also brings profound peace as we step out of the worry we were never meant to carry.

Here are some practical ways to put this into action:

1. **Start Your Day with Surrender**
Each morning, set the tone with a simple prayer: *"Lord, I trust You with today. Guide me, provide for me, and remind me that You are enough for this moment."* When we begin the day by releasing control, we align ourselves with God's pace rather than the frantic rhythm of the world.

2. **Pause Before Overcommitting**
When faced with new opportunities or obligations, pause and ask: *"Is this something God is calling me to today, or am I rushing ahead out of excitement or fear?"* Learning to say no to what doesn't align with God's priorities for the day keeps you grounded and focused.

3. **Let Go of the What-Ifs**
Worry thrives on hypotheticals—what might go wrong, what could happen. Instead of spiraling, remind yourself that God already knows and has equipped you with what you need for today. Trust that He'll meet you in tomorrow's challenges when they arrive.

4. **Break the Habit of Overplanning**
Plan responsibly, but hold your schedule loosely. Rather than mapping out every detail weeks in advance, focus on the tasks and responsibilities God has placed before you today. This practice frees you from the anxiety of trying to control every outcome.

5. **Practice Gratitude for Today's Provision**
Like the Israelites gathering daily manna, focus on the blessings and resources God provides today. End your day by reflecting on three things you're grateful for, shifting your focus from what might happen to what God has already done.

This step, perhaps more than any other, releases us from the exhausting grip of self-reliance. It reminds us that God is the ultimate author of our days, and He holds tomorrow securely in His hands.

Reflection

By trusting Him for every 24 hours, we find peace in the present, joy in His provision, and the strength to face whatever comes next.

1. **In what areas of your life are you most resistant to letting go of control?** Whether it's your schedule, your family's future, or your finances, ask yourself why surrendering these areas feels difficult. What steps can you take to release them to God?

2. **What are you holding onto when it comes to tomorrow?** Take a moment to think about what keeps you up at night. Is it a deadline, a fear of failure, or uncertainty about the future? How might releasing those worries to God change the way you approach today?

3. **How often do you find yourself over-planning or overthinking?** Are you trying to solve problems that haven't even arrived yet? Reflect on how this habit impacts your peace of mind and your ability to trust God with what lies ahead.

Each moment of scripture meditation, gratitude, or stillness becomes an offering, a way of saying, *"Lord, I trust You to transform my mind."*

These questions are designed to help you examine the ways you can release your grip on tomorrow, align your heart with God's provision, and cultivate a life rooted in daily trust.

CHAPTER 8: STEP SIX ESTABLISH BETTER HABITS

I was apprehensive to include this chapter. The term "self-care" has become a trendy buzzword, and it's easy to roll your eyes when it pops up yet again. I get it—there's an entire industry built around the idea of self-care, much of it veering into vanity or consumerism. The enemy loves to twist this concept too, whispering lies that make us feel unworthy. Let me be clear: *no matter your health right now, you are not unworthy.* Your value isn't determined by the state of your body, your fitness routine, or the number of steps on your watch. You are fully loved, fully seen, and fully treasured by God.

That said, we have the *privilege* to choose something good for our bodies today. This isn't about guilt or perfection—it's about stewardship. God gave us our bodies as temples to house His Spirit (1 Corinthians 6:19-20). Taking care of them isn't a punishment or a checklist; it's a way to honor Him. It's not about striving but about partnering with God to do the best we can, one day at a time.

When Healthy Habits Feel Hard

For 11 years, I was a health and fitness coach with Beachbody (now called BODi). If you've read my earlier books, you know that this was a vibrant season of my life. Healthy habits felt like second nature to me back then. Working out, planning meals, and encouraging others to prioritize their health brought me joy. It wasn't just something I did—it was who I was. I loved the people I met, the trips we earned, and the satisfaction of seeing others thrive because of the programs and supplements I recommended.

But in 2022, everything shifted. A doctor I was seeing for adrenal fatigue gave me a prescription I never expected: *rest*. If you've read chapter two, you know the background, so I'll keep it brief. My cortisol levels were out of control, and while my workouts and lifestyle weren't the culprits, my adrenals had taken a beating from years of swallowing big external stresses internally. He strongly encouraged me to pause my workouts, sleep in, and allow my adrenals to heal. Intellectually, it made sense, but emotionally? It felt like a betrayal of everything that kept me grounded. For years, my mornings had been my sanctuary—a sacred combination of a quick devotion, a satisfying workout, and some form of glorious caffeine. It wasn't about pushing limits; it was about maintaining a flow I loved. Suddenly, that flow was gone, and with it, the sense of inertia I didn't even realize I'd been white-knuckling.

I followed the doctor's advice, and over time, my energy improved, my lab results looked better, and physically, I felt healed. But when the doctor gave me the green light to start working out again, something was missing: my motivation. The switch that had always been so easy to flip just… stayed off. This pause wasn't meant to last forever; it was a temporary prescription to heal. And yet, when it was time to get back to it, I couldn't muster the discipline or drive I once had. The routines I used to enjoy felt daunting, and I was left frustrated—wanting to dive back in but feeling stuck in a strange limbo of reluctance.

If you've ever struggled with the cycle of trying and giving up—whether it's a fitness plan, eating better, or getting off the couch—you're not alone. You've tried the group classes, bought the cute leggings, maybe even gone all-in on the latest smoothie trend. And then, somewhere along the way, the honeymoon phase ends. The excitement fades, and you're left wondering, *What's the point?*

Here's the point: when your motivation is rooted in vanity, it's destined to fade. And let me be clear—I'm not saying that's the case for you. Often, our intentions are good, our motives grounded in truth, yet the enemy finds a foothold so deep that we feel stuck, unable to move forward. It's not always about misplaced desires; sometimes it's about the quiet, sneaky ways the enemy works to keep us from the freedom God wants for us. But when your motivation is rooted in obedience to God, you can draw strength from Him. Philippians 2:13 reminds us that *"God works in you to will and to act in order to fulfill His good purpose."* That means He gives us both the *desire* and the *ability* to do what pleases Him. And yes, that includes taking care of the bodies He's entrusted to us.

Instead of viewing healthy habits as a burden or a way to "fix" yourself, what if you saw them as a form of worship? A way to thank God for the gift of your body and to prepare yourself to serve Him more fully? When we prioritize our health, we equip ourselves with the energy, clarity, and perseverance needed to walk in God's calling. It's not about achieving perfection; it's about being faithful with what He's given us.

When I finally shifted my mindset, I realized that small, consistent steps—like drinking more water, taking a daily walk, or starting my morning with prayer—weren't just "good habits." They were opportunities to connect with God and align my life with His will.

Building better habits isn't about self-reliance; it's about surrender. Ephesians 3:20 reminds us that *"God is able to do exceedingly abundantly above all that we ask or think, according to the power that works in us."* That power is already within you, not because of your willpower but because of His Spirit.

This step is about laying down the belief that you have to do it all on your own. It's about asking God for the strength to make one small change today—not out of guilt but out of gratitude. When you take that first step, you'll find that He meets you there, ready to guide and sustain you. As we dive deeper into this chapter, let's focus not on perfection but on progress. Let's reframe healthy habits as acts of obedience, opportunities to glorify God, and tools to help us thrive in the life He's called us to live.

The Blueprint for Consistent Habits

It's easy to feel like life is pulling us in a thousand directions, isn't it? Our schedules, distractions, and constant demands make consistency seem like an unattainable dream. If anyone had a reason to let change dictate their days, it was Daniel.

Living in Babylon, Daniel was immersed in a culture of extravagance and upheaval. The pace was relentless, the pressures unending, and the temptations to conform were everywhere. Yet, in this whirlwind of distraction, Daniel stood out—not because of his wealth, status, or achievements, but because of his quiet, unwavering commitment to habits that honored God.

Daniel's life wasn't defined by reactive moments of faith but by steady, intentional practices that kept him grounded. We see it so clearly in Daniel 6:10: *"Now when Daniel learned that the decree had been published, he went home to his upstairs room where the windows opened toward Jerusalem. Three times a day he got down on his knees and prayed, giving thanks to his God, just as he had done before"* (NIV).

Notice the last part: *"just as he had done before."* This wasn't a new ritual he started in the face of adversity; it was a habit already deeply rooted in his life. Daniel prayed three times a day—not out of convenience or crisis, but out of conviction. Even when a decree made prayer punishable by death, Daniel didn't flinch. His habits were foundational, anchoring him in God's presence no matter what Babylon threw his way.

Reading Daniel's story, I'm struck by how his consistency wasn't dependent on his circumstances. He didn't pray because his life was peaceful, nor did he stop praying when it became dangerous. His habits were so ingrained that they carried him through every season of life, from quiet obedience to literal lion's dens.

And honestly, I envy that kind of discipline. For years, my own habits felt effortless—healthy routines that came naturally, built on years of consistency. But my natural momentum came to a grinding halt. What started as a well-intentioned rest period turned into a prolonged struggle to rebuild the habits I'd once cherished.

Rebuilding habits, I've learned, is less about waiting for motivation and more about making a commitment. It's about following Daniel's example: showing up, day after day, no matter how we feel or what challenges arise. Daniel didn't pray because it was easy; he prayed because it was essential. That's the mindset I had to rediscover—a realization that habits grounded in faith and obedience are vital anchors, not optional add-ons.

The Science of Small Steps

When Proverbs 3:5-6 encourages us to "*Trust in the LORD with all your heart and lean not on your own understanding*," it's not asking us to ignore practical steps. Instead, it's a reminder that while we rely on God for direction and strength, we also take intentional actions that align with His wisdom. This step beautifully marries biblical wisdom with scientific evidence, proving that small, deliberate changes can transform our health, mindset, and faith.

James Clear, in *Atomic Habits*, highlights the incredible power of small, consistent changes. He explains that habits form through a process of cue, routine, and reward, and that small steps compound over time, creating exponential results. For example, committing to just 10 minutes of movement each day can shift your mindset, improve your physical health, and set the foundation for larger changes.

From a neurological standpoint, forming new habits rewires the brain. Each small, repeated action strengthens neural pathways, making the habit easier over time. It's like blazing a trail through a dense forest: the more you walk the path, the clearer it becomes. This is why starting small can lead to transformative changes.

God designed our bodies to respond positively to intentional care. Research consistently shows that small, regular habits, such as moderate exercise, healthy eating, and quality sleep, yield significant mental and physical health benefits. Here are a few science-backed examples:

Exercise: Studies show that as little as 10-15 minutes of physical activity per day reduces anxiety, improves mood by increasing endorphins, and lowers cortisol (the stress hormone). Over time, this consistency strengthens both body and mind, providing resilience against burnout.

Nutrition: Simple swaps, like choosing fruit over sugary snacks, stabilize blood sugar levels, improving energy and focus. These small changes also support better hormone regulation, aiding overall wellness.

Sleep and Rest: Prioritizing intentional rest, even if it's just going to bed 30 minutes earlier, has profound effects. It reduces cortisol levels, sharpens memory, and boosts immune function, all of which combat the symptoms of burnout and adrenal fatigue.

The Biblical Perspective on Small Steps

Throughout Scripture, God demonstrates that He values small beginnings and consistent faithfulness. In Zechariah 4:10, we're reminded, *"Do not despise these small beginnings, for the Lord rejoices to see the work begin."* Similarly, Jesus teaches that even faith the size of a mustard seed can move mountains (Matthew 17:20).

Small steps honor God because they demonstrate trust in His ability to amplify our efforts. They reflect a heart of obedience, faith, and dependence on Him rather than relying on our own strength. When we take purposeful steps toward healthier habits, we align ourselves with the life He's designed for us.

It's easy to feel daunted when starting something new, but the goal isn't perfection—it's progress. Like Daniel's steadfast commitment to prayer, your habits don't have to be grand to matter. Small changes may feel insignificant at first, but they create momentum. Over time, they anchor you in peace and renew your energy for God's purposes. Trust that God doesn't expect you to fix everything all at once. He simply invites you to take the next small step in faith.

Motivation Shift: From Vanity to Obedience

For years, my motivation for maintaining healthy habits was tied to external goals. If I'm being honest, I liked the idea of feeling confident in my clothes, and I enjoyed the compliments that came with it. But here's the thing about vanity: it's like a sparkler at a Fourth of July picnic—it burns bright for a moment but fizzles out before you've even finished marveling at it. Weight loss goals, aesthetics, or fleeting validation might get you started, but they rarely sustain you. And when life throws you a curveball, like sleepless nights, a demanding schedule, or a pandemic (remember that gem?), the spark burns out entirely.

This morning, as I sat down to edit this chapter, I had already procrastinated on moving my body. I woke up early, put on my workout clothes, and even pulled up my computer to stream a prenatal workout. Yes, I'm pregnant with baby #4 while writing this chapter, and let me tell you—this first-trimester stuff is for the birds.

I knew, though, that movement—even a gentle stretch or light exercise—would benefit both me and my baby. It wasn't about crushing an extreme workout or chasing a specific goal; it was about being faithful with the body God has entrusted me with. And honestly? The motivation wasn't there. But I also knew that the words I was about to edit would lose their integrity if I didn't apply these practices to my own life. So I plowed through the excuses, hit play on the workout, and stretched out on the mat, knowing it was a small but meaningful step of obedience.

It's in these everyday choices that we move from striving to surrender. God equips us with the power to persevere. When we shift our focus to honoring Him through our habits, we're no longer bound by fleeting motivations or the enemy's whispers of inadequacy. We're free to pursue health and wellness as an act of worship, trusting that He will meet us in our weakness and multiply our efforts.

And let's be real—this is a journey I'm still on with you. Some days, the snooze button wins. Other days, I lace up my shoes and push through, not because I feel like it, but because I trust that God is shaping me through these small acts of obedience.

Real-Life Application: Turning Healthy Habits into Acts of Obedience

Shifting your mindset from self-reliance to God-reliance through healthy habits isn't about suddenly becoming a fitness expert or transforming into someone who thrives on bland protein shakes and marathon training. It's about cultivating small, purposeful routines that care for the temple God entrusted to you, while inviting Him to be the source of your strength.

Here's how to begin:

1. **Start Small and Be Consistent**

Rome wasn't built in a day, and your habits won't be either. Pick one thing you can commit to now—join a gym, walk a mile, or spend ten quiet minutes with God before your family realizes you're awake. Science shows that small, consistent steps build lasting habits, and Proverbs 16:3 reminds us, *"Commit to the Lord whatever you do, and He will establish your plans."* So if your plan involves less couch time and more walking around the block, trust God to meet you there—even if the block feels more like a marathon right now.

2. **Connect Your Habits to Your Faith**

Think of your morning workout as a way to survive... I mean, thrive through your kids' energy levels. Eating an extra veggie? That's stewarding the body God gave you, not a punishment for that second brownie last night. When you tie your actions to obedience rather than appearances, you'll find joy in even the smallest habits. Remember, the goal is to honor God with what you've got (which might include sore muscles and mismatched socks).

3. **Prioritize Rest and Recovery**

If God took a break on the seventh day, you can, too. Rest isn't a luxury; it's a necessity. That might look like a power nap, going to bed earlier, or saying "no" to the 23rd commitment on your calendar this week. Exodus 14:14 says, *"The Lord will fight for you; you need only to be still."* So put down the laundry basket for a minute.

4. Embrace Accountability

You don't have to do this alone. Find a friend who'll lovingly remind you not to raid the cookie jar at 11 p.m. (again). Share your goals and celebrate the wins—like drinking an entire glass of water without spilling it. Ecclesiastes 4:9-10 says, *"Two are better than one because they have a good return for their labor: If either of them falls down, one can help the other up."* Or, in modern terms, one can stop the other from eating an entire bag of chips "accidentally."

5. Release the Burden of Perfection

God isn't keeping a workout log or calorie counter on you. When you miss a workout or devour an entire pizza instead of a salad, give yourself grace and remember Philippians 1:6: *"He who began a good work in you will carry it on to completion."* Perfection is overrated; progress is the real win. Plus, Jesus didn't call perfect people—He called faithful ones.

6. Lay Down Tomorrow's Worries

Matthew 6:34 says, "*Do not worry about tomorrow, for tomorrow will worry about itself.*" Translation: today's task is to choose one good thing for your body or mind and trust God with the rest. Tomorrow can handle itself—preferably without the stress you're carrying from today.

Healthy habits are about being equipped to live out God's calling with strength, clarity, and joy. Whether you're starting with baby steps or full lunges, each choice is an act of obedience that honors Him. Grab your water bottle, lace up your sneakers, and give yourself grace.

Reflection

You're doing this for His glory, not your Instagram followers. And that, my friend, is something worth showing up for.

1. **What motivates your current habits?**
Are they driven by a desire to honor God, or do they stem from external pressures like appearance, comparison, or cultural trends? How might shifting your motivation to obedience and stewardship impact your ability to sustain them?

2. **What is one small habit you could start today?**
Think about a realistic, actionable step you can take that aligns with honoring God through your body and mind. What would it look like to prioritize progress over perfection?

3. **What excuses are holding you back from prioritizing your health and well-being?**
How can you surrender those to God, trusting Him to equip you with the energy and motivation to make better choices?

4. **How can your habits reflect trust in God rather than reliance on yourself?**
Reflect on how releasing control and letting God guide your routines could transform the way you approach self-care and healthy living.

5. **Who can you invite to support and encourage you in your journey?**
Whether it's a family member, friend, or small group, who could help you stay accountable and celebrate small wins as you build sustainable, God-centered habits?

As you begin to build habits that honor God and prioritize your well-being, you might notice resistance—not just in your schedule or circumstances but in your own mind. Change is hard, and our thought patterns can often be the biggest roadblocks to embracing new rhythms. That's where the next step comes in: rewiring your brain.

If you've struggled to fully implement any of these steps, don't worry. You're not alone, and you're not stuck. God designed our minds with the incredible capacity for growth and renewal. Neuroplasticity—our brain's ability to create new pathways—is a real thing, and it aligns perfectly with biblical principles. *"Do not conform to the pattern of this world, but be transformed by the renewing of your mind"* (Romans 12:2).

In the next chapter, we'll dive into how you can retrain your thoughts, overcome mental obstacles, and align your mindset with God's truth to live out these principles fully and joyfully. Get ready to see how powerful your mind—and God's transformative work within it—can be.

CHAPTER 9: STEP SEVEN- REWIRE YOUR BRAIN

The pen hovered over my journal as my mind raced faster than I could write. Thoughts of unfinished tasks, parenting challenges, and everything in between jostled for space in my brain. It felt like trying to organize a junk drawer while someone kept tossing more random items in—overwhelming and utterly impossible.

Years ago, this feeling wasn't the result of a bad day; it was a pattern. My mental hamster wheel spun endlessly, and no matter how fast I tried to run, I couldn't escape the feeling that I was falling short. *Take every thought captive?* Sure, Paul. I couldn't even take my own attention span captive. How was I supposed to turn this mental chaos into anything remotely resembling obedience to Christ?

If that sounds familiar, you're in good company. We live in a world that thrives on multitasking. We juggle careers, relationships, family obligations, and personal growth, all while fielding a constant barrage of notifications, reminders, and endless demands. Rest feels like a luxury we can't afford, and stillness? Practically extinct. The result? Frazzled minds that crave peace but can't find the way out of the noise.

Here's the good news: you're not stuck here. God never intended for us to live on the edge of burnout, our thoughts running wild like untamed horses. He offers us a better way—a way to reclaim our minds and renew our spirits. *"We take captive every thought to make it obedient to Christ"* (2 Corinthians 10:5, NIV). This verse isn't a suggestion; it's a promise. It reminds us that we have the power, through Christ, to shift our mental patterns, find calm, and create a life that reflects His peace.

Before we dive into this final step, let's take a moment to reflect on how far we've come. If you've made it to this chapter, you've already done some heavy lifting. You've explored what it means to find your own *Gilgal*, that sacred space of rest and reset. You've recognized the beauty and necessity of leaning on others instead of trying to carry life alone. You've identified your energy leaks, learned to let go of control, established healthier habits, and embraced the freedom of living one day at a time. Each of these steps has been intentional, helping you shed the weight of burnout and self-reliance.

But external changes, no matter how meaningful, can only take you so far if your thought life is still spinning out of control. True transformation starts from the inside out. While the previous steps have prepared you to manage the external factors, this final step is about going deeper—addressing the root of the struggle, the patterns of thinking that keep you tethered to stress, worry, and striving.

This chapter isn't a bow to wrap everything up neatly; it's the key to making it all stick. Rewiring your brain is what takes these steps from fleeting attempts at change to permanent ways of living in God's peace. It's the shift from managing your circumstances to transforming how you respond to them.

The journey so far has been about recognizing God's presence in the practical and external; now, it's time to fully embrace Him in your internal thought patterns. This is where the real transformation begins.

We'll explore what it means to rewire your brain—to intentionally create mental habits that honor God and help you find rest in Him. It's not an overnight fix or a flashy self-help strategy. It's a process, one thought at a time, one prayer at a time, one moment at a time.

The Science of Neuroplasticity and Biblical Renewal

Let's start with a word that sounds like it belongs in a sci-fi movie: *neuroplasticity.* Before you roll your eyes and think, *Great, now it's going to get super boring* – hang tight—it's simpler than it sounds and way cooler than you might expect.

Neuroplasticity is the brain's ability to adapt and rewire itself based on repeated thoughts and actions. In other words, your brain is like a path through a forest. The more you walk a particular route—whether it's a pattern of worry, gratitude, or obsessive Googling of your symptoms at 3 a.m.—the more defined that path becomes. The good news? You can forge new trails. The bad news? If you've been hiking the "Stress and Self-Doubt Loop" for years, it's going to take some rerouting.

Here's where it gets interesting—and, frankly, a little convicting. Many of us unknowingly train our brains to be really good at stressing out. Every time you spiral over a work email, overthink a text message, or mentally replay that awkward thing you said three years ago, you're reinforcing the neural pathways for anxiety and self-doubt. Your brain becomes an expert in worry because, well, you've been coaching it.

But like we can train our brains to stress, we can also train them to trust. And this isn't some new-age, self-help mumbo jumbo; it's backed by science *and* scripture. God designed our brains to be moldable, adaptable, and, ultimately, aligned with His truth.

Romans 12:2 lays it out perfectly: *"Do not conform to the pattern of this world, but be transformed by the renewing of your mind."* Think of this verse as the biblical explanation of neuroplasticity. God is saying, "*Hey, those thought patterns that keep you stuck? They don't have to own you. You can create new ones—ones rooted in peace, trust, and My promises.*"

Every time you pause to pray, meditate on scripture, or take a deep breath instead of losing your cool, you're laying down new mental tracks. You're teaching your brain to take the scenic route to peace instead of the shortcut to panic. It's like replacing a pothole-riddled dirt road with a smooth, paved highway—but it takes consistency and patience.

I'll admit, the process isn't instant. If you've been overthinking and overworking for years, your brain isn't going to suddenly transform overnight. You might have moments where your old habits rear their ugly heads (like when your kid spills their drink on your laptop and you temporarily forget Jesus said *anything* about grace). But with each intentional step—whether it's a whispered prayer in the middle of a disaster or a scripture verse sticky-noted to your bathroom mirror—you're rewiring your brain.

God, the ultimate Creator, designed our brains with an incredible ability to change because He knew we'd need it. He knew we'd mess up, stress out, and spiral into thought patterns that feel impossible to escape. In His infinite wisdom, He gave us the capacity for renewal—a chance to reset and redirect our minds toward truth and peace. And here's the part that might blow your mind: science has studied this. Experts suggest that it takes an average of 66 repetitions to form a new habit or neural pathway. That means every time you pause, every time you choose to dwell on godly thoughts or pray instead of spiraling, you're laying another brick on the path toward mental transformation.

Let's be real, 66 times doesn't sound easy. And let's be even *more* real—sometimes it feels impossible. Abruptly changing your attitude and thought life? That's not just hard; it's nearly unbearable on your own strength. Here's the million-dollar question: *Is rewiring your brain really something you're supposed to do alone?* The answer is a resounding no.

God's Word makes it clear that transformation isn't about self-reliance—it's about divine reliance. Philippians 2:13 reminds us, *"For it is God who works in you to will and to act in order to fulfill his good purpose."* The ability to change your thoughts and reset isn't about gritting your teeth and muscling through. It's about trusting the God who wired your brain in the first place. Yes, we participate in the process by taking captive our thoughts (2 Corinthians 10:5) and meditating on what is true, noble, and praiseworthy (Philippians 4:8). But the power to succeed comes from Him, not us.

If you've ever tried and failed to change your thinking, you are not a failure. You are not weak. You're human, and that's why this final step isn't about trying harder—it's about surrendering more. God doesn't expect you to navigate this transformation alone. He is the One who equips you with the power, self-control, and grace to rewire your mind (2 Timothy 1:7).

The next time you feel overwhelmed, remember that your brain was made to change, but the ultimate work of transformation belongs to God. Every small, intentional action you take is a step of faith, an offering He uses to pave new paths in your mind. And the most comforting truth? He's not just helping you rewrite your story; He's walking alongside you every step of the way. It's humbling—and a little awe-inspiring—to think that the Creator of the universe is also the greatest neuroscientist.

If you're looking for an example of true transformation, Saul's journey to becoming Paul stands out as one of the most remarkable in history. This wasn't a minor adjustment or a simple change in behavior—it was a complete renewal of his thoughts, habits, and purpose. Saul, a man driven by pride, anger, and misguided zeal, became one of the greatest advocates for Christ through God's power. If God could work that level of change in Saul, He can work in us as well.

The Cost of Not Renewing Your Mind

Picture your mind as a garden. What you plant will grow, and what you neglect? That becomes a tangled, overgrown mess of weeds. An unchecked mind operates the same way—old, negative thought patterns creep in like invasive vines, strangling peace, joy, and spiritual vitality. Left untended, anxiety takes root, self-doubt blooms, and exhaustion grows unchecked. Weeds don't ask for permission; they take over. Renewal, on the other hand, requires intentionality, diligence, and, most importantly, reliance on God.

Nowhere is this lesson more vividly illustrated than in the life of Saul of Tarsus. Before his transformation into Paul, the apostle we revere today, Saul's mind was dominated by rigid legalism, pride, and a misguided sense of religious zeal. Fueled by anger and self-righteousness, Saul was on a mission to persecute Christians, convinced that he was defending the faith. His mind was like a garden overtaken not by passive neglect but by the aggressive thorns of hatred.

But God had other plans. On the road to Damascus, Saul was stopped in his tracks by a blinding light and the voice of Jesus Himself (Acts 9:1-19). This was the starting point of a complete overhaul—an intense season of mental, spiritual, and emotional renewal. Stripped of his vision and his sense of control, Saul spent three days in darkness, grappling with the reality that everything he believed was wrong. The scales falling from his eyes marked more than physical healing—it was the rebirth of his perspective, values, and identity.

Saul didn't become Paul in an instant. That miraculous moment was the catalyst, but Paul's letters reveal that his transformation was a daily act of surrender. In Romans 7:15-25, Paul openly admits his ongoing struggle: *"For I do not do the good I want to do, but the evil I do not want to do—this I keep on doing."* Even Paul, one of the greatest champions of the faith, wrestled with the weeds of old habits and thoughts. But he didn't stay there. In Philippians 3:13-14, we see his determination to move forward: *"Forgetting what is behind and straining toward what is ahead, I press on toward the goal to win the prize for which God has called me heavenward in Christ Jesus."*

What does this mean for us? It means that transformation isn't a one-time event; it's a lifetime journey. Like Paul, we must continually surrender our minds to God, allowing Him to replace old thought patterns with His truth.

I've experienced the cost of neglecting this renewal process. Seasons of burnout, exhaustion, and doubt crept in when I allowed my mind to dwell on lies like, *"You're not enough"* or *"You have to do it all on your own."* These thoughts didn't only affect my mood; they infiltrated my actions, relationships, and spiritual life. I tried to fight back with self-help methods, productivity hacks, and sheer determination, but nothing brought lasting peace. It wasn't until I invited God into the mess, surrendering my need for control, that real change began.

When negative thought patterns go unchecked, they cloud our clarity, steal our peace, and make it harder to hear God's voice. The impact isn't limited to our emotions; it affects our spiritual well-being too. Trust gives way to anxiety, and striving takes over where surrender belongs.

But here's the beauty of God's grace: He doesn't leave us to fend for ourselves. He steps into our overgrown mental gardens with the tools we need to start fresh. He pulls out the weeds of worry and comparison, tills the soil of our hearts, and plants seeds of peace, joy, and truth.

Saul's transformation into Paul is a profound reminder that God's renewal isn't surface-level; it's complete. The same God who rewired Paul's mind is eager to do the same for you.

What's growing in the garden of your mind? Are there thoughts choking out the peace God promises? Are there lies that need uprooting? You don't have to tackle it alone. Invite the Master Gardener in. Trust Him to cultivate a mind that reflects His truth, one thought at a time. Because when you do, you'll find that His peace is deeper, His love is wider, and His transformation is greater than you ever imagined.

Real-Life Application to Rewiring Your Mind

Rewiring your brain is about small, intentional steps that align your thoughts with God's truth and peace. Each of these practices offers a tangible way to bring renewal into your daily life, transforming your mindset over time.

1. **Daily Scripture Meditation**

Start your day by anchoring your thoughts in God's Word. Philippians 4:8 reminds us to dwell on what is *"true, noble, right, pure, lovely, admirable."* By focusing on these truths, you train your brain to seek God's goodness even amid chaos.

How to Start: Choose one verse each morning—perhaps Philippians 4:8 or Romans 12:2—and meditate on it during a quiet moment. Repeat the verse aloud as you take a morning walk or sip your coffee. Let its truth sink in, guiding your thoughts for the day.

Why It Works: Scripture meditation helps form new mental pathways that lead to peace and trust in God. Neuroplasticity research supports this: repeated focus on positive, life-giving truths reshapes your brain over time.

2. **Gratitude Journaling**

Gratitude is a powerful tool for rewiring your perspective. Writing down three things you're thankful for each evening—even small things like a kind word or a warm cup of tea—shifts your focus from what's wrong to what's right in your life.

Biblical Backing: 1 Thessalonians 5:18 urges us to *"give thanks in all circumstances."* Gratitude isn't about denying challenges but recognizing God's faithfulness within them.

How to Start: Keep a notebook by your bed. Each night, jot down three things that made you smile, brought comfort, or reminded you of God's presence. Over time, this habit rewires your brain to default to gratitude instead of negativity.

3. Intentional Breathing and Prayer

When stress rises, your body reacts—but you can counter it by engaging both your mind and spirit. A simple breathing exercise paired with prayer can calm your nervous system and re-center your thoughts on God.

How to Practice: Inhale deeply for four counts, then exhale slowly for four counts. As you exhale, pray something simple like, *"Lord, You are in control."* Repeat this for a few minutes whenever you feel overwhelmed.

Biblical Backing: Psalm 46:10 invites us to *"Be still, and know that I am God."* Pausing to breathe and pray helps you embody this stillness, even in the midst of life's demands.

4. Digital Detox Periods

Our minds are constantly bombarded by information, notifications, and distractions. Stepping away from screens creates space for clarity, reflection, and connection with God.

How to Start: Designate specific times during the day to unplug. Maybe it's an hour in the morning or before bed, or even a full day each week. Use this time for scripture, prayer, or simply being present with loved ones.

Biblical Parallel: Saul's three days of blindness were a forced detox, stripping away distractions and creating space for God to reshape his heart and mind. Use your detox periods as intentional pauses to listen for God's voice.

5. **Choosing Slow**

The world pressures us to move faster, achieve more, and check off endless to-do lists. But renewal often comes in the still moments, when we choose to slow down and savor the gifts God has given us.

How to Practice: Try activities that invite slowness and reflection. Savor your meals instead of rushing through them. Take a walk without your phone and notice the beauty around you. Spend time journaling or sitting quietly in prayer.

Biblical Backing: Elijah encountered God not in the powerful wind or earthquake but in the gentle whisper (1 Kings 19:12). Slowing down allows us to hear God's still, small voice in our own lives.

These practices are about partnering with God, allowing Him to work through your intentional efforts.

Reflection

Each moment of scripture meditation, gratitude, or stillness becomes an offering, a way of saying, *"Lord, I trust You to transform my mind."*

1. **What thought patterns in your life feel most out of control or overwhelming?** Identify areas where negativity, worry, or self-reliance dominate. How can you invite God into these specific struggles to begin the process of renewal?

2. **Are you currently "watering weeds" in your mental garden?** Consider what thoughts or habits might be choking out peace and joy. What steps can you take this week to replace those with God's truth?

3. **When was the last time you intentionally paused to meditate on scripture or reflect on God's goodness?** How could you incorporate daily moments of gratitude or prayer into your routine to cultivate new, healthier thought patterns?

4. **What role does surrender play in transforming your mind?** Reflect on areas where you're trying to control outcomes or rely on your own strength. What would it look like to let go and trust God to do the work of renewal in you?

5. **How can you apply the concept of neuroplasticity to your spiritual life?** Think about one small, consistent practice you can commit to that aligns with God's promises— whether it's scripture meditation, gratitude journaling, or intentional breathing and prayer. How might this shape your thoughts and habits over time?

6. **Do you believe God is able to transform your mind completely?** If not, what doubts are holding you back? Take a moment to pray and ask Him to replace those doubts with faith in His power to renew and restore.

These questions help you pause, reflect, and take practical steps toward a renewed mind that aligns with God's peace and purpose. You don't have to fix everything all at once; you just need to start. And with every step, know that God is faithful to complete the good work He began in you (Philippians 1:6).

CHAPTER 10: THE JOURNEY BEYOND BURNOUT

There's a peculiar cocktail of emotions that comes with stepping back into life after burnout. It's part hesitant tiptoe, part hopeful leap, and entirely nerve-wracking. It feels like standing at the edge of a high dive, wondering if the water below will catch you or sting like a belly flop gone wrong. I vividly remember sitting at my kitchen table one quiet morning, staring at my planner as if it were a live grenade. On one hand, a little voice in my head whispered, *You've got this! You're ready!* On the other hand, a louder, more obnoxious voice screamed, *Abort mission! Too much danger ahead!*

My life, fresh from the wreckage of burnout, had settled into a new tempo of peace and purpose, and for the first time in a long while, I could breathe. But as I stared at those empty spaces on my calendar, the thought of filling them felt like inviting overwhelm all over again. What if I couldn't keep up? What if I slipped back into those same old patterns of striving and self-reliance? What if all the calm I had worked so hard to cultivate unraveled faster than my kids' attention spans?

The thing about re-engagement after burnout is that it's not just about logistics—it's emotional. You're torn between wanting to step back into the life God has called you to and fearing that life might eat you alive. It's a tension between hope and hesitation, excitement and trepidation. And if you've been there, you know exactly what I mean.

But as I sat there, pen hovering above that blank planner page, something clicked. The answer wasn't about dodging life altogether or wrapping myself in bubble wrap labeled *Fragile: Handle With Care.* It wasn't about finding the perfect formula for balance—because, spoiler alert, balance is a myth invented by people who never had kids or deadlines. No, the answer was in how I approached life. It wasn't about diving back in fearlessly; it was about leaning on Jesus as my strength and letting Him set the boundaries for what was good and right in this new season.

Letting Go of DIY Faith

As I stared at that planner on my kitchen table, I realized something unsettling: I was trying to map out a life that looked eerily like the one that had burned me out in the first place. Sure, I was wiser now—at least, I hoped so—but old habits have a sneaky way of showing up, dressed as "necessity" or "opportunity." It was a little too easy to start thinking, *I've got this. I can handle it.* But if burnout taught me anything, it's that self-reliance is a fast train to exhaustion.

The temptation to rely on our own strength is as old as the garden of Eden. Remember Adam and Eve? They had everything they needed, straight from God's hand. But the moment they believed the lie that they could take control and do it better, everything unraveled. And isn't that the cycle we find ourselves in, too? We convince ourselves we're strong enough, smart enough, or capable enough to handle life without leaning fully on God—until the cracks start to show.

When stepping back into life after burnout, the greatest danger isn't the demands themselves; it's the mindset that says, *I have to figure this out on my own.* This isn't about avoiding responsibility or playing the victim; it's about recognizing the difference between carrying a yoke of grace and dragging a boulder of self-imposed pressure.

Jesus knew how easily we slip into striving, which is why His words in Matthew 11:28-30 are a lifeline:

"Come to me, all you who are weary and burdened, and I will give you rest. Take my yoke upon you and learn from me, for I am gentle and humble in heart, and you will find rest for your souls. For my yoke is easy and my burden is light."

Did you catch that? His yoke is easy. His burden is light. But we often try to exchange it for the heavy, back-breaking load of our own plans, timelines, and expectations. Leaning on God isn't a sign of weakness; it's an act of wisdom.

When I hit burnout, I realized how much I had been relying on my own understanding. I'd pray for guidance but then rush to solve things my way, living in a constant state of DIY faith. Post-burnout, setting boundaries meant reevaluating every "yes." It wasn't about clearing my calendar—it was about clearing my heart. Why was I saying yes? Was it guilt, hype, or obligation, or was it genuinely God's leading? If it wasn't aligned with His call, it became a no—even when saying no felt uncomfortable.

Setting Boundaries and Guardrails

Guardrails are the practical side of boundaries. They're the tangible habits, schedules, and reminders that keep us from veering back into the ditch. For some, it's scheduling intentional Sabbath rest each week. For others, it's committing to not checking emails after 8 p.m. But one of the most important guardrails we can set is regularly evaluating how long it's been since we've spent time in our *Gilgal*—that sacred space of worship, rest, and reset (remember this from step one?). For me, creating margin in my day became less about crossing items off a to-do list and more about making room to breathe, reflect, and reconnect with God. When I neglect my Gilgal, everything else starts to slide. But when I intentionally return to that place, I'm reminded of His promises and equipped to face life's demands without losing my footing.

Remember Nehemiah, tasked with the monumental job of rebuilding the walls of Jerusalem? He faced relentless distractions and opposition, from mockery to outright threats. Yet, his focus remained unshaken. When critics tried to lure him away with their schemes, his response was resolute: *"I am doing a great work and I cannot come down"* (Nehemiah 6:3). Nehemiah understood his mission and knew that stepping away—even for a moment—could jeopardize the work God had called him to.

That's the kind of focus we need when re-engaging with life, especially after burnout. But here's the thing—Nehemiah wasn't just running on grit. He had a system in place: workers stationed with tools in one hand and weapons in the other, a community standing guard over each other's progress (Nehemiah 4:17-18). He wasn't doing it alone, and neither should we. Guardrails, much like Nehemiah's setup, are what help us stay "on the wall," doing the work God has called us to without being pulled away by every demand, expectation, or shiny distraction.

This is where *Gilgal* comes in. Think of it as your spiritual checkpoint, a space to pause and remember why you're on the wall in the first place. Just as Nehemiah's workers needed to take shifts, we need to evaluate regularly how long it's been since we've spent time in our own Gilgal—our place of worship, rest, and recharging. Without it, we risk losing sight of the bigger picture and getting swept up in the noise of life.

And let's not forget accountability. Nehemiah had people beside him, ready to sound the trumpet when danger arose (Nehemiah 4:20). We need those people too—friends, mentors, or family members who can call us out when we're veering off course. Guardrails aren't about avoiding distractions; they're about ensuring we stay rooted in God's strength, equipped to keep moving forward without falling into old patterns. With these structures in place, we can confidently say, like Nehemiah, *"I am doing a great work and I cannot come down."*

Leaning on God doesn't mean we're passive bystanders. It means we're active participants in His work, equipped by His strength, guided by His wisdom, and sustained by His peace. Setting boundaries and trusting God with the rest isn't about playing it safe; it's about stepping boldly into the life He's called us to, knowing we're not walking alone.

As I sat there that day, when I felt frozen that I didn't know how to navigate real-life without falling back into bad habits, I made a decision: I wouldn't fill those empty spaces with tasks born out of fear or pride. I'd let God fill them—with His peace, His purpose, and His pace. And when I did, something remarkable happened. The pressure eased. The hamster wheel slowed. And for the first time in a long time, I felt free.

That's the power of the shift from self-reliance to God-dependence. When we let God hold the pen, the story always turns out better than we could have imagined.

Faithfulness Over Perfection

After burnout, fear often creeps in like an unwelcome guest, whispering lies that make us question everything. The "what ifs" seem louder and more convincing than ever. *What if I fail again? What if I overcommit and exhaust myself? What if I end up right back where I started?* These fears feel valid because they echo real pain from past experiences, but they don't have to define you. Failure, exhaustion, and even relapse aren't your identity. Your identity is rooted in God's faithfulness, not your circumstances.

The enemy thrives on using fear to paralyze us, crafting lies that keep us from moving forward. Fear insists we have to protect ourselves from every potential disaster, but Scripture interrupts that narrative. In 2 Timothy 1:7, we're reminded: *"For God has not given us a spirit of fear, but of power and of love and of a sound mind."* Fear isn't from God—it's a weapon of the enemy, designed to keep you from stepping into the freedom and purpose God has for you. The good news? God has already overcome fear. You don't have to muster the strength to overcome it alone; you simply need to trust the One who already holds victory over it.

Think about Peter stepping out of the boat. Fear didn't magically disappear before he walked on water. The waves didn't settle, the wind didn't hush, and Peter didn't suddenly become invincible. What got Peter out of the boat wasn't fearlessness; it was trust. He focused on Jesus and took one step at a time. That's the key for us too, especially after burnout. You don't need to fix everything all at once. You don't need to take giant leaps. Small, consistent steps of obedience—one choice at a time—are enough.

What might your first step look like? Maybe it's saying "no" to one more obligation, carving out intentional Sabbath rest, or giving yourself permission to stop striving. Maybe it's as simple as opening your Bible for five minutes each morning or reaching out to a trusted friend for prayer and accountability. Whatever it is, don't underestimate the power of starting small. God asks for faithfulness, and He promises to meet you exactly where you are.

This brings us to a crucial shift in how we define success. The world bombards us with the message that success is measured by how much we do, how many achievements we collect, and how efficiently we manage our to-do lists. But God's definition of success is vastly different. It's not about the quantity of our accomplishments—it's about the quality of our relationship with Him.

For us, this means redefining success as faithfulness rather than productivity. It's not about spinning every plate perfectly or impressing others with how much we can juggle. Success is aligning our hearts with God's will, walking in obedience, and trusting Him to guide the outcomes. It's about focusing on *His* work instead of our own striving.

Take a moment to ask yourself: *What does obedience look like for me in this season?* For some, it might mean stepping into something new that feels scary but aligned with God's call. For others, it might mean resting or stepping back to regain your footing. Either way, success isn't about what you accomplish; it's about how faithfully you follow His leading.

When we trust God with the outcomes, the pressure lifts. The weight of "what if" fades, replaced by the assurance of His sovereignty. He isn't grading you on how well you avoid mistakes or how much you achieve. He's inviting you to trust Him with the journey, to take small steps of obedience, and to rest in His promise that *He* will complete the good work He started in you (Philippians 1:6).

As you face the “what ifs” and wrestle with redefining success, remember this: you don’t have to have it all figured out. Your job isn’t to eliminate fear but to keep walking forward, even if fear lingers at the edges. Success isn’t reaching the finish line in one triumphant leap—it’s trusting Jesus in each small step. Focus on Him, and you’ll find that His faithfulness is enough to carry you toward peace, purpose, and rest.

Here’s something we don’t often consider: peace is a weapon. It’s not passive; it actively dismantles the chaos the enemy throws your way. In Ephesians 6:15, Paul describes peace as part of the armor of God, calling it the *“readiness that comes from the gospel of peace.”* This readiness means that peace equips you to stand firm, even when life feels like a battlefield.

Think about Jesus sleeping in the boat during the storm (Mark 4:35-41). While the disciples panicked, Jesus rested, fully confident in His authority over the storm. When He stood and rebuked the wind, peace didn’t just calm the waves; it silenced fear and restored faith. That’s the kind of peace God offers us—a peace that doesn’t just soothe but empowers. When you stay anchored in God’s peace, you’re equipped to face life’s storms with courage, knowing that His presence is stronger than any wave.

As we close this chapter, consider what it would look like to keep your focus on Jesus in this new season. Just as Peter found solid footing on the water when his eyes were fixed on Christ, you’ll find the strength and peace you need when your gaze remains on Him. How can you anchor your heart in His promises as you navigate the uncertainties ahead?

Take courage in knowing that the God who calls you is faithful. He doesn't promise a path without waves, but He does promise to hold you steady through them. Trust Him with your fears, your focus, and your steps forward.

CHAPTER 11: CONCLUSION

Here we are. You've made it to the end of this book—congratulations! If you're anything like me, you've probably read this while juggling a lukewarm cup of coffee and at least one child calling your name in the background. Or maybe you've stolen away for a rare moment of quiet, whispering a prayer that no one finds you. Either way, *you did it.* You've walked through every chapter, reflected on every question (hopefully), and now you're staring at the finish line, wondering, *Okay, now what?*

Let me be clear: finishing this book doesn't mean you've "arrived." There's no heavenly confetti waiting to rain down on you (although I wouldn't mind that every now and then). This isn't about achieving a final destination; it's about learning how to live differently, how to embrace rest not as a break between burnout cycles but as a way of life.

Returning to Your Gilgal

Yep, Gilgal again. That sacred place where the Israelites paused, reflected, and recalibrated. We talked about it way back at the beginning. I've mentioned it so much that you might even be tempted to roll your eyes, but hear me out: *your Gilgal is everything.*

Let's be real: life never actually "slows down." You've seen the meme, right? The one that says, "Being an adult is saying, 'Things will slow down in a few weeks,' over and over until you die." It's funny because it's true. So if you're waiting for the perfect moment to rest or reflect, it's not coming. That's why your Gilgal matters. It's your intentional pause—a sacred pit stop to remember God's faithfulness, recalibrate your priorities, and prepare for what's ahead.

Here's the thing about rest: it's not the finish line; it's the foundation. It's the steady ground beneath your feet as you step into the work, relationships, and purpose God has called you to. Rest isn't passive; it's active trust in the One who holds it all together.

Isaiah 41:10 says, *"Do not fear, for I am with you; do not be dismayed, for I am your God. I will strengthen you and help you; I will uphold you with my righteous right hand."* That's not just a nice sentiment to cross-stitch on a pillow; it's a promise. God equips you to rest. He strengthens you, helps you, and upholds you. When the waves rise or the demands of life pull at you, He's the anchor that keeps you steady.

Rest isn't just for you. When you live from a place of peace, it spills over into the lives of those around you. Your family, your friends, your coworkers—they all benefit from a version of you that's grounded, intentional, and connected to God's presence.

Staying anchored in God's peace overflows into your relationships, your work, and your ministry. People are drawn to peace because it's so rare in our frantic, fast-paced world. When you live from a place of deep, abiding peace, it becomes a testimony to God's power at work in your life.

Think about Paul and Silas singing hymns in prison (Acts 16:25). Their circumstances were anything but peaceful—beaten, chained, and sitting in a dark cell—but their peace wasn't rooted in their situation. It was rooted in their Savior. And because of that, their worship led to the miraculous salvation of the jailer and his family. Your peace has the power to inspire others to seek the source of it for themselves.

Your Turn to Walk

As we close this journey together, let's pause and reflect on the seven steps we've walked through:

Step 1: Identify Your Gilgal – Discover the place where you can meet with God, reset, and find clarity.

Step 2: Build Your Circle – Surround yourself with people who encourage, sharpen, and carry you in the hard moments.

Step 3: Stop Wasting Energy – Identify what's draining you and learn to focus on what truly matters.

Step 4: Be Willing to Give It All Up – Surrender everything—your plans, your dreams, your striving—to God's perfect will.

Step 5: Live a 24-Hour Life – Embrace today without worrying about tomorrow. Trust God's provision moment by moment.

Step 6: Establish Better Habits – Cultivate daily practices that honor God and steward the body, mind, and spirit He's given you.

Step 7: Rewire Your Brain – Renew your mind by replacing lies with God's truth and building a mindset rooted in His grace.

What do you do with everything you've read, reflected on, and wrestled with in these pages? You take it with you—not as a heavy burden but as a guide. You keep coming back to the truths God has revealed, and you let them shape how you live.

Will you mess up? Of course. You'll have days where the "yes" slips out before you think, or where you binge-watch an entire season of TV instead of opening your Bible (been there). But that's okay. God is a God of mercy.

Take the next step. Return to your Gilgal. Set those boundaries. Trust God's timing. And most of all, remember that He's with you every step of the way. The God who invites you into rest is the same God who equips you to carry His peace into a world that desperately needs it.

And if all else fails, just take a nap. Seriously. Sometimes the holiest thing you can do is rest your body and trust that the world will keep spinning without you.

This journey isn't a sprint; it's a lifelong walk with a faithful God who never grows weary. He's not asking you to get it all right the first time or to fix yourself overnight. He's asking you to walk with Him, to trust Him, and to let Him shape your heart through every step of the process.

Take what you've learned, weave it into your daily walk, and let God guide you on the path to rest. You've got this—not because of your strength, but because of His. Step forward in faith, anchored in the promise that He is with you, He is for you, and He will complete the good work He's begun in you.

"When you trust God with your limits, you discover His limitless power."

ACKNOWLEDGMENTS

To my husband, Nick: Thank you for listening to me talk through the ideas in this book for years, helping me solidify the details of our stories and offering insights that made this message stronger. Thank you for bringing me hot tea on those early mornings while I worked at the dining table

And to my kids: You're my constant source of entertainment and joy. Thank you for inspiring me to write books and for the laughs and lessons we've shared along the way. I've loved sharing the truths of *The Path to Rest* during our home Bible studies.

To my mom, Missy Hawkins: You've always told me I could do anything I put my mind to. Thank you for reading everything I've written and for your sharp eye that has caught countless typos and grammatical errors. Your love and encouragement have been the wind beneath my wings.

To my literary agent, Michelle Lazurek at WordWise Media: Thank you for believing in me and giving a new author a chance. Your support has been invaluable, and I'm deeply grateful for your guidance.

To my writing coach, Amanda S. Bacon: Your expertise and encouragement during the 2020 Book Proposal Bootcamp with Lysa TerKeurst gave me the tools I needed to refine this message. Thank you for helping me shape these lessons into something I could confidently share with the world.

To my advanced readers: Thank you for your feedback, reviews, and unwavering support in sharing this book with your circles. Your help has been a vital part of this launch, and I couldn't have done it without you.

To my blog readers, both new and old: You've blown me away this past year with your incredible support as our readership has grown by astronomical percentages. Thank you for sticking with me, for reading, and for finding value in the words I share.

And to my blog coach, Laura Peters: Thank you for showing me the backend of blogging with clarity and patience. You've turned something technical and intimidating into something fun and achievable, and your guidance has been a game-changer for me.

To my God and Savior: You are the root and reason for all of this. Thank You for giving me the words to write and the grace to learn as I go. Thank You for teaching me patience and faithfulness.

With gratitude,
Laura

ABOUT THE AUTHOR

Laura Mendenhall is a writer, speaker, and intentional living advocate with a heart for helping women slow down, prioritize what matters, and align their lives with God's purpose.

With a seminary degree in Small Group Discipleship and as the best-selling author of *Love Fast Live Slow*, Laura blends biblical truth with practical tools to inspire faith, rest, and meaningful connections.

From navigating burnout to juggling motherhood and homeschooling, Laura's story is real, relatable, and rooted in grace. She lives near Atlanta with her husband, Nick, and their three (soon to be four!) children, finding joy in baking sourdough, teaching at her homeschool co-op, and leading small groups at church.

Her latest book, *The Path to Rest*, offers a biblically grounded roadmap to overcoming burnout and living with peace and purpose. Connect with Laura at www.lovefastliveslow.com or laura@lovefastliveslow.com.

CHECK OUT LAURA'S OTHER BOOKS

Love Fast Live Slow: Discover the Simplicity of Reflecting Jesus in a Stressful World

Bible Hero Devotional Series:

Unsung Heroes: How Faithful Mothers in the Bible Overcame Battles to Make a Generational Impact

Almost Heroes: How God's People Can Ruin a Good Thing

Hidden Heroes: How God Uses Everyday People to Change the World

Manufactured by Amazon.ca
Acheson, AB

15422860R00087